NUBANK
PURPLE REVOLUTION

THE STORY BEHIND THE FINTECH
THAT TRANSFORMED BANKING

NUBANK
PURPLE REVOLUTION

THE STORY BEHIND THE FINTECH
THAT TRANSFORMED BANKING

JORGE LIVINGSTONE

Title:
NUBANK PURPLE REVOLUTION
THE STORY BEHIND THE FINTECH
THAT TRANSFORMED BANKING

Original Title in Spanish:
NUBANK REVOLUCIÓN MORADA
LA HISTORIA DETRÁS DE LA FINTECH
QUE TRANSFORMÓ LA BANCA

Copyright © 2024 Jorge Livingstone Vaught

ISBN: 9798334939899
First Edition Aug 2024 (v1g)
All Rights Reserved.

Legal Notice and Disclaimer
This book is not affiliated, sponsored, approved, or authorized in any way by NU Holdings Ltd. or any of its affiliated companies. All trademarks and logos mentioned or depicted in this book are the property of their respective owners and are used solely for identification and commentary purposes. The use of these names, trademarks, and logos is made under the doctrine of fair use and is intended to provide journalistic, historical, and educational context about NUBANK and its development.

The author and publisher have made every effort to ensure the accuracy of the information contained in this book. However, no responsibility is assumed for errors, omissions, or misinterpretations of the contents. The opinions expressed in this book are solely those of the author and do not necessarily represent the views of NU Holdings Ltd. or its employees, directors, or affiliates.

No part of this book may be reproduced or incorporated into a computer system, or transmitted in any form or by any means, electronic, mechanical, by printing, photocopying, recording, or other methods, without the prior written permission of the copyright holder: jorgelv@mac.com

TO MY BELOVED WIFE
AND OUR CHILDREN,
WHO ARE MY INSPIRATION
AND STRENGTH

Index

- INDEX 7
- PREFACE 11
- NUBANK 21
- ORIGINS OF NUBANK 27
  - DAVID VÉLEZ 27
  - COLOMBIA 28
  - COSTA RICA 32
  - SAN FRANCISCO 37
  - STANFORD 40
  - NEW YORK 44
  - BRAZIL 45
  - SEQUOIA CAPITAL 48
  - THE IDEA 57
  - MARIEL REYES MIL 60
  - SEQUOIA LEAVES BRAZIL 63
  - THE BANK BRANCH 64
  - TRADITIONAL BANKING 67
  - THE BANKING MODEL CAN CHANGE 72
  - THE PITCH DECK 75
  - STRATEGIC ADJUSTMENTS 86
  - THE FIRST INVESTOR 87
  - FOUNDATION OF NUBANK 91
  - THE HOUSE ON RUA CALIFORNIA 92
  - THE CREDIT CARD 95
    - *The Purple Card* 96
    - *Payment Processing* 97
    - *The Journey of the App* 98
    - *The Launch Test* 101

TRACTION 103
    The Waiting List Strategy *105*
LIQUIDITY CRISIS 107
THE BRAZILIAN BANKING LICENSE 112
MEXICO 114
    Growth *117*
    Investment and Expansion *118*
COLOMBIA 123
    Product Expansion *125*
    Challenges and Future *127*

THE CO-FOUNDERS 131

CRISTINA JUNQUEIRA 131
EDWARD WIBLE 140

NUBANK'S IPO 145

    The Great Leap *145*
THE INFLUENCE OF ANITTA 149

CULTURE AND VALUES OF NUBANK 151

CULTURE 151
    Where Do We Want to Go? *153*
VALUES 156
VISION AND MISSION 158
THE NU BRAND 159
    Nubank's Visual Renewal *160*

NUBANK FANS 163

DIFFERENT TYPES OF CUSTOMERS 163
NUBANK CUSTOMERS 164
CUSTOMER SERVICE 166
THE XPEERS 167
MARKETING CAMPAIGNS 171
CUSTOMER ACQUISITION COST 173
    Nubank's CAC *174*

>   *Organic Marketing*......175
>   *Net Promoter Score* 176
> THE NPS 176
>   *Calculating the NPS:* 177

PRODUCT INNOVATION 181

> NUBANK'S FIRST PRODUCT 182
>   *The Credit Card* 184
>   *Caveat Emptor* 185
> A TALE OF INNOVATION AND PRUDENCE 188
>   *The Purple Card* 189
>   *The Influence of Capital One* 190
> NUBANK PRODUCTS 195
>   *The Ultravioleta* 196
>   *Checking and Savings Account* 199
>   *Foreign Exchange Market* 201
>   *New Services* 203
>   *Nubank Shopping* 204
>   *Digital Personal Banker* 206
> CONSUMER PROTECTION 207
>   *Scalability and Security* 207
>   *Modo Rua* 208
>   *Me Roubaram* 209
> FINANCIAL INCLUSION 210

NU TECHNOLOGY 215

> SECURITY AT NU 219
> TECHNOLOGICAL RISKS 223

MANAGEMENT AND OPERATION 225

> NUBANKERS 225
>   *NU Rituals* 230
>   *Experience Over Time* 233
> ORGANIZATIONAL STRUCTURE 236
> THE BOARD 236

INGENIOUS PATH TO PROFIT 239

　THE NU MODEL 239
　THE CREDIT CARD BUSINESS 241
　　Interchange Fees 244
　　Credit Card Payment Process 246
　　Payment Processing Fees Structure 248
　　Importance of Interchange Fees 248
　　Interest Income 248
　　Delinquency Rate 249

CAPITALIZATION 251

　FINANCING 254
　INVESTMENT ROUNDS 255
　FUNDING THE FUTURE 258

CHALLENGES 263

　A ROCKY ROAD 263
　WE ARE THE BEST 264
　STRATEGIC AND OPERATIONAL RISKS 266
　FINANCIAL REGULATION 268
　NAVIGATING REGULATION 269

THE PURPLE REVOLUTION IN RETROSPECTIVE 271

ANNEXES 275

　ANNEX 1 276
　ANNEX 2 277
　ANNEX 3 280
　ANNEX 4 284
　ANNEX 5 285
　ANNEX 6 286

ABOUT THE AUTHOR 287

Preface

Given Nubank's highly successful trajectory, I decided to create a business case about this fintech, similar to the one I wrote about the Apple Card credit card for my business students. While researching, I came across the business case that Michael Chu wrote for the Harvard Business School in 2020, titled "Nubank: Democratizing Financial Services."[1] However, four years had passed since then, during which Nubank had made many significant advances. Since that time, Nubank had not only tripled in size and capitalization but also expanded its customer base from 33.7 million to 100 million.

I began gathering information for my case, seeking data and testimonials. To my surprise, I found an abundance of information about Nubank's founders: between two and three dozen interviews with David Vélez, both in video and written form, along with several more featuring Cristina Junqueira and Edward Wible. These were available in Spanish, English, and, as expected, many in Portuguese. Without realizing it, I no longer had a simple case in my hands; it had evolved into such an intriguing story that I could not bring myself to cut it down. It was a compelling topic that I felt I had to share with my colleagues and students.

Since its founding in 2013, Nubank has not only challenged the traditional norms of the financial sector but has

---

[1] Chu, Michael, et al. Harvard Business School. Business Case 9-321-068. Rev. Aug 2023. "Nubank: Democratizing Financial Services"

effectively rewritten them, forever revolutionizing the way people interact with banking services.

With a perfect blend of innovative technology and unparalleled customer service, they have created something truly remarkable, like modern-day "aurifices,"[2] turning ideas into gold. Nubank has transformed financial services, making them not only accessible and efficient—directly benefiting users as never before—but also enjoyable, placing the customer at the heart of the business. While these basic principles of 21st-century marketing might seem obvious, it is surprising that no traditional bank had taken the initiative to implement them.

While studying Nubank, I was constantly reminded of Steve Jobs' thought-provoking speech at Stanford University on June 12, 2005[3], where he spoke about "connecting the dots."[4] I am not sure if David Vélez had the chance to be present at that speech, but the essence of Jobs' words resonates strongly when analyzing Nubank's trajectory. Every decision, every innovation, and every step Nubank took seems to fit together seamlessly. If we connect the dots, we can begin to understand how the three founders were able to create something as remarkable as Nubank.

---

[2] An aurifex is an alchemist who specializes in the transmutation of common metals into gold, using esoteric practices and knowledge in the quest for the philosopher's stone.
[3] Stanford University. 2005. "Steve Jobs' 2005 Stanford Commencement Address"
https://youtu.be/UF8uR6Z6KLc?si=wyt-p0cdnPhTYtZt
[4] The phrase "*connecting the dots*" by Steve Jobs comes from his commencement speech at Stanford University in 2005. In this speech, Jobs shared a reflection on how seemingly unrelated events in his life came together to create the path that led to his success. The main idea behind this phrase is that in life, we often cannot foresee how current decisions and experiences will influence our future. The dots (events, decisions, experiences) may not always make sense while we are living them, but when looking back, we can see how they connect and form a coherent trajectory.

Steve Jobs spoke about how the milestones—or dots—of our lives, seemingly disconnected in the present, often come together in surprising and significant ways in the future. But he warned that *you can only connect the dots looking backwards*. As humans, we are not always insightful in our actions or decisions; we move forward according to our goals and circumstances of the moment. The true revelation comes when we look back and see a path we never imagined.

Allow me to turn back time a bit and shift the focus.

Digital banks and all other fintechs that exist are possible thanks to the smartphone and the Internet. The real smartphone, as we know it today, was the one Apple launched in 2007.

It is clear to me that Steve Jobs understood the iPhone's potential perfectly from the moment he conceived it. However, I was struck by how he introduced it to the public in January 2007. Jobs emphasized that the iPhone was three products in one: a powerful iPod with a touch screen, a revolutionary mobile phone, and an innovative Internet device.[5] But in reality, the iPhone was the most powerful computer ever created at that time, operated with one hand, and fit in your pocket. Its user interface was entirely revolutionary, with the invention of multi-touch, and its software gave it unparalleled potential, as the iPhone ran on the same operating system as a Mac. This changed everything.

Jobs' commercial strategy had a clear marketing purpose. Simply saying, *I present to you the smallest computer in the*

---

[5] Villacorta, Juan Carlos. May 2018. "16 años iPhone: Presentación primer iPhone 2007 por Steve Jobs". https://www.youtube.com/watch?v=R-sLPTUEq6E&t=139s

world, probably would not have had the same impact. Among other things, because the iPhone at that time only had three significant active applications: the iPod, the phone, and Safari—the mobile browser—along with some additional tools like the calculator and the camera.

However, there was much more behind this invention. It represented a powerful business concept, supported by all the necessary software tools to bring it to life, and backed by a robust infrastructure.

The arrival of smartphones, along with faster versions of the Internet, and catalyzed by Samsung's blatant copying of Apple's invention, changed the world.

This shift paved the way for the emergence of true digital banks like Nubank.

Returning to the story of Nubank, I have conceptually divided it into two parts:

The first part focuses on the trajectory of its founder, who, whether consciously or not, prepared from a very young age to eventually create Nubank. He also skillfully found his two partners, who amplified his ability to bring Nubank to life.

The second part delves into Nubank itself—what makes it so unique, so compelling. This is due to the essence, the soul that was infused into it, resulting in an entity with a true personality of its own, perfectly structured, with goals and principles that set it apart from any other digital bank in the world.

It is obvious that Nubank is much more than a powerful mobile application.

Among the many digital banks and fintechs that have emerged in recent years, I believe that few truly understand that success transcends the app that launched them. While the application is undeniably important, serving as the bank's branch and the public face of the institution, the real key lies in the spirit that drives them. It is the "soul" behind the application that truly makes the difference. David Vélez understood this from day one.

When observing various aspects of David's life—such as the practical advice he received from his parents, his family upbringing, his academic training, the jobs and bosses he encountered in different financial institutions—every decision, every reaction to adversity, every challenge overcome, and every innovation implemented seem like dots that, when connected, reveal how he prepared for his ultimate goal. A series of experiences, seemingly isolated at the time, gave David the strength to embark on this difficult and complex adventure.

In an interview, when asked if he had plans to start a new venture, David, with great candor, responded:

No, I'm very tired, out of energy,

David admitted with a bittersweet smile,

I sleep like a baby, but I wake up every 3 hours crying, in panic, in bed. I have very demanding days, it's brutal, all this takes a gigantic psychological toll, I couldn't.[6]

---

[6] Restrepro, Claudia. Universidad EAFIT. Entrevista con David. Oct, 2022. "Educación, liderazgo y tecnología".

That statement does not surprise me at all; it has been an exhausting endeavor. From what little I have been able to learn, he and his co-founders have faced countless challenges, crises, setbacks, and slights that are not visible to the public. Meanwhile, his company, partners, and shareholders demand perfection at every turn.

Nubank has burst into the banking sector and taken it by surprise—not because people were unaware of its presence, but because traditional banks underestimated and ignored it. However, the fact is irrefutable: Nubank has rewritten the rules of traditional banking forever.

Nubank is the *sharpest pencil in the box* in the financial sector. By any metric used to evaluate its performance as a fintech, it surpasses others by far and has done so since its early years. The correct metrics to assess its performance now are those typically applied to traditional banks. Even by these standards, Nubank, in its mere 10 years of operation—since 2014, when they launched their iconic purple card—has consistently outperformed long-established institutions.

NU boasts the highest Net Promoter Score (NPS) in the financial sector. In 2024, the industry benchmark was 30,[7] yet Nubank in Mexico achieved a score of over 96,[8] reflecting a

---

https://youtu.be/RXznpOGKwNM?si=HNmyXDmUU-4x2AM-

[7] Reileanu, Greg. Mar 2024. RETENTLY, "What is a Good Net Promoter Score? (2024 NPS Benchmark)" https://www.retently.com/blog/good-net-promoter-score/#:~:text=A%20score%20between%200%20and,happy%20customers%20than%20unhappy%20ones

[8] Nubank, Redacción. Aug 2022. "Net Promoter Score de NU: Amamos saber qué piensan nuestros clientes" https://blog.nu.com.mx/net-promoter-score-de-nu-amamos-saber-que-piensan-nuestros-clientes/

unusually high level of customer satisfaction for a financial institution.

In terms of customer numbers, Nubank surpasses all banks except the Asian giants, with more than 100 million customers and only 7,000 employees to serve them.[9] To put this in perspective, BBVA has 74.1 million customers worldwide and 121,000 employees.[10]

Learning about the three founders of Nubank has been both an interesting and extremely rewarding experience. Their sharp vision and disruptive strategies are remarkable, but much of their success can also be attributed to their rigorous and careful preparation, along with the dedication, sacrifice, and perseverance they have invested to achieve it.

I believe we cannot overlook the incredible luck that has accompanied them throughout their journey. It is impressive. However, for those who do not believe in luck, as Louis Pasteur rightly said, *"Luck favors only the prepared mind,"* A Latin adage attributed to Virgil also reminds us that fortune favors the bold: *"Fortuna audaces iuvat."* Indeed, there is luck, aiding the prepared and the bold... aiding them on their journey.

In the interviews given by David, Cristina, and the fewer by Edward, they all show a simple and humble attitude, but at the same time, they exhibit strong realism and great energy. They are fully aware that their mission is not yet complete and hint that

---

[9] Nubank, Sobre NU. Nuestros datos. Jun 2024.
https://international.nubank.com.br/es/sobre-nu/
[10] BBVA. Información corporativa. 2023.
https://www.bbva.com/es/informacion-corporativa/#:~:text=BBVA%20es%20un%20grupo%20financiero,y%20más%20de%20121.000%20empleados.

there is still much more to come. They always emphasize how much they still have to innovate, thus preventing Nubank from becoming complacent.

From what I have seen and heard from David, it feels as though I have known him my entire life. I can sense when he is happy, when he is visibly tired, when he grows irritated with the interviewer, or when he is relaxed and enjoying the conversation. I have even observed how the years have marked him.

When founders speak about their companies, they usually recount only what the public wants to hear: the successes and the great battles won. But they seldom talk about all the suffering, the exhausting moments, and the painful setbacks they endured, because that material is not as compelling. Entrepreneurs often do not share these stories, or they downplay or gloss over them, but they are there, and they are usually quite harrowing.

And well, let's not even mention if the entrepreneur failed in his or her goal, because then there is no one who wants to listen. It happens exactly as Cristina Junqueira said in an interview:

> *Today, everyone thinks it's cool and nice — talking about startups—they only see them on magazine covers and read success stories. No one sees what it really takes... No one talks about all those who failed; there's a famous saying that goes: 'the cemetery of the failed is very quiet.'*[11]

---

[11] The phrase is paraphrased from a passage by Nassim Taleb in his book *The Black Swan*: "The graveyard of failed persons will be full of people who shared the following traits: courage, risk taking, optimism, et cetera. Just like the population of millionaires. There may be some differences in skills, but

Of all the companies that died and **were left behind, no one talks about them.** *People* **only see** *the success stories and think* **everything is** *wonderful. They only see the success,* **without** *considering the cost, how hard the road* **was, and** *how many sacrifices were made along* **the way.**[12]

In summary, this book is a chronicle of **the journey the founders took to create Nubank, and it is also a recognition of the vision of David, Cristina, and Edward.**

It is an invitation to all entrepreneurs and **those with great aspirations to believe in their ideas, to persevere despite how difficult the goal may seem, and to endure all the adversities they must face. Achieving this requires working tirelessly—yes, working until exhaustion—and... a good dose of luck. All to contribute, even a little, to making this world a better place.**

I hope you enjoy this fascinating story **as much as I enjoyed learning about Nubank and its founders, who, with their ingenuity and determination, transformed the financial landscape.**

Jorge Livingstone
Coyoacán, Mexico City, 2024

---

what truly separates the two is for the most part a single **factor: luck. Plain luck."**

[12] Cfr. InvestNews BR. May 2023. "Nubank mira em alta **renda e Inteligência** Artificial, diz Cris Junqueira".
https://www.youtube.com/watch?v=b2q9BXkXkcQ

Nubank

In 2024, the company founded by David Vélez, Cristina Junqueira, and Edward Wible is making headlines worldwide. Amidst comments, interviews, analyses, critiques, applause, and even skepticism about its success, Nubank continues to leave its mark. Over these 11 years, it has diligently done its homework at its own pace. And with each milestone achieved, they celebrate and share it with the world—well deserved!

By July 2024, Nubank had reached a market capitalization of $60.3 billion, surpassing the vast majority of traditional banks and potentially becoming the largest digital bank. With over 100 million customers and consistent growth, quarter after quarter since its inception, it is an unstoppable force in the banking sector. In 2023, it generated a total revenue of $7.729 billion.

Nubank was founded on May 6, 2013, with a clear and bold mission:

> *Combat the complexity of banking to empower people in their daily lives by reinventing financial services.*[13]

Nubank's model is more than validated and has enormous growth potential. In Latin America alone, which consists of 33 countries, there is a market of over 670 million people.[14] Nubank

---

[13] Nubank. https://international.nubank.com.br/es/sobre-nu/
[14] In 2024, the total population of the 33 countries in Latin America and the Caribbean is approximately 669.7 million people. Here are some of the most

is already present in Brazil, Mexico, and Colombia,[15] and has so far captured 15% of this total potential market in the region.

Nubank is a digital bank—a challenger bank, to be precise—though David Vélez, its founder, often emphasizes that *more than a bank, we are a technology company that happens to be in the financial sector.*

The terminology surrounding digital banks can be confusing, but understanding how each institution emerged can provide clarity. A startup specializing in the financial sector automatically transitions from a startup to a fintech, becoming a financial technology company. Nowadays, with increased regulation, some type of license granted by a regulator is likely required to be officially considered a fintech. This fintech could take the form of a digital wallet or a crowdfunding platform.[16]

In the evolution of fintech into a bank, there are two possible paths: one involves a financial institution offering digital services created by an existing bank and operating under that bank's license—this is known as a Neobank.

---

populous countries in the region: Brazil: 216.4 million, Mexico: 128.5 million, Colombia: 52.1 million, Argentina: 45.8 million, Peru: 34.4 million, Venezuela: 28.8 million, Chile: 19.6 million, Ecuador: 18.2 million, Guatemala: 18.1 million

[15] Brazil has 216 million inhabitants, of which 92.4 million are its customers. Mexico has 128 million inhabitants, with 6.6 million customers. Colombia has 52 million inhabitants, with 1 million customers.

[16] Crowdfunding is a form of collective financing where a company, project, or idea receives small contributions from a large number of people, usually through the Internet. These platforms allow companies to obtain funds directly from the public, either in exchange for rewards, shares in the company, or simply as donations.

The other path occurs when a fintech directly obtains a banking license, thus becoming a Challenger Bank.

Therefore, a Digital Bank is either a Neobank or a Challenger Bank that can legally engage in financial intermediation, meaning it has a banking license and operates without physical branches, conducting all transactions through a system or application.

It is estimated that there are more than 200 digital banks,[17] but only 30 have reached unicorn status, with valuations exceeding $1 billion. Of these, only five have gone public: Nubank, SoFi, Kakao, Tinkoff, and Judo Bank.

Strictly speaking, due to its founding date of May 6, 2013, Nubank is not the first digital bank in the world; it is the seventh. (See Appendix 1)

The first place belongs to Tinkoff, the Russian bank established in 2006 by entrepreneur Oleg Tinkov. Tinkoff operates without physical branches and offers a wide range of financial services through its online platform and mobile app. Tinkov engineered a remarkable entry into the credit card market. In 2007, a year after its founding, he sent 500,000 invitations by mail to potential customers, offering credit cards with attractive terms. This bold and innovative marketing campaign resulted in a massive response and quickly established Tinkoff as a significant player in the Russian financial market.

The second digital bank, founded in 2009, is Simple Bank, an American bank that began operations in 2012. It was

---

[17] Scasserra, Alejandro. "Challenging. Cómo hacer producto en un banco digital y construir las finanzas del mañana" Buenos Aires. 2022.

acquired by BBVA USA two years later, and both were closed in 2021.[18]

Ally Bank,[19] also founded in 2009, is in third place, followed by SoFi, N26, Kakao, and Nubank.

Nubank began operating in Brazil as a Payment Institution. Over the years, it obtained its banking license in January 2018, becoming one of the youngest members of the venerable global banking club.

On May 17, 2019, Nubank entered the Mexican market, adopting the name NU due to local regulations. In 2021, it expanded into Colombia and took the opportunity to completely redesign its brand, further modernizing it and using both names interchangeably.

In December 2021, Nubank took another significant step by beginning to trade on the New York Stock Exchange under the name NU Holdings, using the ticker symbol NU.

The story of Nubank is a testament to how innovation and a customer-centric approach can redefine a sector as traditional as banking. Since the Medici in the 15th century, who established

---

[18] BBVA USA was a U.S. company and a subsidiary of the Spanish bank BBVA, headquartered in Birmingham, Alabama, until it was acquired by PNC Financial Services in 2021.

[19] GMAC (General Motors Acceptance Corporation), founded in 1919, offered financial services to General Motors customers and dealerships. In 2009, GMAC Bank transformed into Ally Bank, focusing on being a direct-to-consumer bank offering a wide range of financial products, such as savings accounts, checking accounts, certificates of deposit, and auto loans. Its transition to a digital bank allowed Ally Bank to provide banking services without physical branches, leveraging technology to offer convenience and accessibility to its customers.

the first "modern" principles of banking, little had changed in traditional banking. The technological advancements adopted by banks had mostly been certain automations of practices that had been in place for centuries.

To put NU's growth into perspective, let's compare it to BBVA. Although it's a rough comparison, it serves to highlight the fintech's rapid expansion. Notably, the amount of assets held by BBVA's customers is immense compared to NU's customers. However, it is important to consider that NU's strategy focuses on volume.

Comparative Table between Nubank and BBVA

2024	Nubank	BBVA[20]
Foundation	2013	1857
Countries	3	25
Customers	100 million	72 million
Employees	8,000	121,500
Market Value	$60.3 billion	$64.64 billion
Assets	$22 billion	$300 billion
Gross Income	$8.03 billion	$63.77 billion
Net Income	$1.03 billion	$7.67 billion
Income/Employee	$128,875 USD	$63,128 USD

These comparisons reveal the operational efficiency and innovative business model of Nubank. Despite being a much younger entity with fewer employees, Nubank has achieved

---

[20] About BBVA. BBVA. "Información corporativa".
https://www.bbva.com/es/informacion-corporativa/#:~:text=Al%20crecer%20rentablemente%2C%20hemos%20podido,ustedes%2C%20nuestros%20casi%20800.000%20accionistas

significantly higher productivity per employee[21] compared to BBVA.

Just as it did in Brazil, Nubank has already applied for its banking license in Mexico.

---

[21] The "productivity per employee" index measures a company's efficiency by relating its sales or revenue to the number of employees. It is calculated by dividing total sales by the number of employees. This index indicates how much revenue, on average, each employee generates and is used to evaluate performance and labor efficiency within a company.

Origins of Nubank

David Vélez

David Vélez Osorno, the eldest child in his family, was born on October 2, 1981, in the vibrant and prosperous city of Medellín, Colombia. He grew up with his two younger sisters in an environment rich with devotion, dynamism, and entrepreneurial spirit.

David holds a deep affection for the lively and close-knit atmosphere of his home. His father, the eldest of twelve siblings, and his mother, one of six, both came from families steeped in entrepreneurship, where each of his aunts and uncles ran some sort of business.[22] This constant entrepreneurial activity infused their household with energy and a steady buzz of excitement.[23] Conversations about business and discussions of commercial strategies were a daily occurrence at the family table, shaping his curious and ambitious mind from an early age.

---

[22] Knox, Fortt. Entrevista. Aug 2023. "David Velez, Nubank CEO: A Fortt Knox Conversation" https://www.youtube.com/watch?v=8ml4yfyut6o
[23] Stanford Graduate School of Business. Entrevista. May 2022. "David, Founder and CEO of Nubank" https://www.youtube.com/watch?v=23ND-uMh-io&t=82s

The environment in which David was raised was full of life. The blend of hard work and constant responsibility became ingrained in his character from a very young age, instilling values that would stay with him throughout his life.

The anecdotes David shares make it evident that his family's teachings instilled in him a strong work ethic and unwavering determination.

Colombia

From a young age, David exhibited an insatiable drive for autonomy and independence. He vividly recalls his constant activity; by the age of five or six, he was already seeking ways to be useful, even taking on tasks like shining shoes. One of his most cherished memories is the time he offered to help his father in the family's button factory, which produced buttons for denim pants. Whether it was to keep him occupied, his fascination with buttons, or both, his father, undoubtedly pleased by his initiative, made arrangements for the very young David to assist.

The task likely involved sorting broken or deformed buttons or anything that did not meet the factory's quality standards. It was a perfect activity for an energetic and detail-oriented child like him, allowing him to feel even more connected to the family's work environment.

David remembers this experience vividly, and in many interviews where this memory comes up, he recounts it with pride. He always emphasizes how much he enjoyed the opportunity to help out and be available for whatever was needed.

In one of those interviews in 2022 at his alma mater, Stanford University,[24] David fondly recalled the environment in his family, where participation was key. In his household, everyone was heard—always—and everyone was eager to help solve any situation. David remarked, *it was always about leading and not necessarily following rules.*[25] In his family, questioning rules that did not make sense and creating opportunities to solve problems was almost a family sport.

This questioning mindset, along with his ability to see beyond established norms and the education he received in an environment that valued participation and leadership, combined with his early practical experiences, formed the foundation of his personality. His capacity to challenge the status quo was cultivated in a home where questioning rules was common practice.

The various anecdotes David shares about his childhood offer insights into his restlessness, boundless curiosity, and energy, and how he channeled these traits. For instance, like a true millennial, he was already fascinated by computers at a young age. Around the age of seven, he enrolled

---

[24] Cfr. Stromeyer, Christopher, Entrevista. Stanford Graduate School of Business. May 2022. Insight by Standford Business. Entrevista con David. https://www.gsb.stanford.edu/insights/david-velez-position-yourself-scarcity-not-oversupply

[25] Cfr. Stromeyer, Christopher, Entrevista. Stanford.

in a two-week summer course at the "Children's University"[26] of EAFIT[27] because he wanted to learn about computing. There, he took a programming class in Logo.[28]

As David grew older, he remembers earning a few "pesos" by washing cars. It was a family environment *where hard work was not only valued but expected*.[29] There was always work to be done, situations to resolve, or difficult problems to face.

As the years passed, by the late 1980s, the situation in Colombia began to deteriorate significantly, largely due to the rise of drug trafficking. Medellín was experiencing severe social fragmentation and rapidly increasing inequality. Violence and a high homicide rate became part of daily life and conversation. The poorest communities, especially those on the urban peripheries, lived in extreme vulnerability and

---

[26] Restrepro, Claudia. Universidad EAFIT. Entrevista con David. Oct, 2022. "Educación, liderazgo y tecnología".
https://youtu.be/RXznpOGKwNM?si=HNmyXDmUU-4x2AM-
[27] Universidad EAFIT (originally the acronym for Escuela de Administración, Finanzas e Instituto Tecnológico) is a private Colombian university. Its main campus is located in the southern part of Medellín, in the El Poblado neighborhood.
[28] The Logo language is a programming language primarily designed for education. It was developed in the 1960s by Seymour Papert and others at MIT. Logo is known for its simplicity and its ability to teach programming and mathematical concepts in a visual and playful manner. It uses a "turtle" that moves on the screen, leaving a trail that allows users to draw shapes and geometric patterns. The commands in the Logo language are simple and intuitive, making it easy to use for teaching children and beginners the fundamentals of programming.
[29] Cfr. Conferencia de David, Universidad de Antioquia. Sep 2023. "Hablemos sobre emprendimiento de alto Impacto".
https://www.youtube.com/live/dxmxUQHAips?si=xc1JBQLOJ4RqcJlB

marginalization. The neglect of infrastructure and basic services exacerbated their plight as drug trafficking infiltrated many aspects of daily life.[30]

Particularly in the capital, violence and corruption were rampant. The power of the Medellín Cartel, led by Pablo Escobar, grew significantly, influencing all aspects of political and social life. Escobar used his economic power to buy influence and secure protection for his drug empire. The drug wars and internal cartel struggles turned Medellín into one of the most dangerous cities in the world at that time.

David vividly recalls a terrifying experience: the entire family had gone on an outing to a shopping mall. As they were leaving, purely by chance, they exited just minutes before a bomb exploded. However, the final straw for the Vélez family was the kidnapping and subsequent rescue of one of David's uncles. At the time, David was about eight years old.

After these traumatic episodes and considering various destinations, the family decided to migrate to Costa Rica in 1990.[31] With suitcases full of hope and a bit of fear, they left the chaos behind to seek a new beginning in safer lands. A new adventure began.

---

[30] López Díez, Juan Carlos. El Eafitense. Edición 105. Feb 2017. "La década del terror (Los años ochenta).
https://www.eafit.edu.co/medios/eleafitense/105/Paginas/la-decada-del-terror.aspx

[31] Cfr. Valora Analitik. Finanzas Personales. Apr 2021. "Las 4 lecciones empresariales de David para el mundo".
https://www.valoraanalitik.com/las-4-lecciones-empresariales-de-david-velez-para-el-mundo

This migration represented a drastic but necessary change for the Vélez family. In Costa Rica, they found a safer and more stable environment where the family could continue to thrive in a less hostile setting. This move provided them with a true respite from the terrible violence that plagued Medellín.

Costa Rica

They arrived in the city of San José on a rainy afternoon, to their new home—a smaller house compared to the one they had in Medellín. It marked the beginning of a new adventure for everyone: discovering a new city, making new friends, and adapting to a new school. The transition was smooth and serene. Costa Rica, with its stable and developing economy and a culture deeply focused on family values, made it easier for the Vélez family to adjust. The neighborhoods were quiet and safe, with paved streets and accessible basic services. The sense of community and neighborly interactions were common and valued aspects of daily life.[32]

David's father relocated his denim jeans button factory to San José, quickly adapting to the new life. In this city, education was highly valued, and participation in extracurricular activities was strongly encouraged. David, who had attended a German school in Medellín, continued his studies at another German-speaking school in Costa Rica.

---

[32] Cfr. Vega, Isabel, et al. "Realidad Familiar en Costa Rica. Aportes y desafíos desde las Ciencias Sociales" FLACSO. Facultad Latinoamericana de Ciencias Sociales. Sede Costa Rica. Ene 2001.
https://biblio.flacsoandes.edu.ec/libros/digital/44274.pdf

David adapted to the new school without any problems and developed a deep love for learning. He was fascinated by languages, admired his teachers, and was a cheerful and polite boy with an innate ease for conversation and a genuine interest in others, naturally standing out as a leader. Changing countries is always a challenge, but it seems David managed to adapt over time. Initially, his different accent made him feel like a foreigner, but gradually that feeling faded, and his *paisa*[33] identity merged with that of a *tico*.[34]

A social studies teacher encouraged David to participate in extracurricular activities, student associations, and sports teams like soccer and swimming. This additional motivation helped him integrate more quickly and rebuild a new life in Costa Rica, taking full advantage of the opportunities that came his way.

For a decade, David immersed himself in the martial art of Tae Kwon-Do, a sport that instilled in him the discipline of

---

[33] *"Paisa"* is a term used to refer to people from the Antioquia region in Colombia. The term is derived from "paisano," which means countryman or compatriot. Paisas are known for their distinctive cultural traits, including a unique accent, traditional cuisine, and a reputation for being industrious and entrepreneurial. The Paisa region encompasses the departments of Antioquia, Caldas, Risaralda, and Quindío.

[34] *"Tico"* is a colloquial term used to refer to people from Costa Rica. The term originates from the local habit of using the diminutive "-tico" instead of the more common "-ito" suffix in Spanish. For example, instead of "momentito" (little moment), Costa Ricans often say "momentico." Ticos are known for their friendly and peaceful nature, as well as their emphasis on education and environmental conservation.

a modern Hwarang.[35] Of course, as a pre-teen, there were days when he would have preferred to be anywhere but the dojang. Yet his mother, with the firmness of a general on campaign, would remind him, *do what you have to do, even if you do not want to*.[36] The couch, playing, or even reading were more tempting options, but his mother, with unwavering determination, emphasized that a commitment is a commitment, and it had to be honored.

Thus, amidst tropical rains and sunny afternoons in the heart of Costa Rica, David forged his character and determination. This rigorous discipline, instilled by his family and reinforced through Tae Kwon-Do training, shaped David in many ways. It taught him not only to be consistent and disciplined but also to value effort and dedication in every aspect of his life. These principles undoubtedly contributed to his personal and professional growth, making David someone who does not easily give up.

Unintentionally, David learned to master his body, pushing it with discipline to do what needed to be done. Self-control became his ally, a crucial skill in combat situations where, despite taking hits, he had to remain calm and respond

---

[35] The *Hwarang* were an elite group of young warriors from ancient Korea, specifically during the Silla Kingdom period (57 BC – 935 AD). The word "Hwarang" means "flower men" or "flower knights," and these youths were selected not only for their martial prowess but also for their nobility, beauty, and moral virtues. The Hwarang are remembered in Korean history as patriotic heroes and symbols of bravery, honor, and commitment to their country.

[36] Cfr. Knox, Fortt. Entrevista. Ago 2023. "David Velez, Nubank CEO: A Fortt Knox Conversation"
https://www.youtube.com/watch?v=8ml4yfyut6o

with precision. This practice not only strengthened his body but also tempered his mind, keeping it in perfect health.

Over time, David achieved a black belt in Tae Kwon-Do. But he did not stop there. He went on to compete on Costa Rica's national team, excelling by winning not one, but two national championships.

During the summers, David continued helping his father in the factory, participating in quality control and working with the machines. He saved all the money he earned. He enjoyed the work environment and the experience he was gaining.

The family had a small country house where David's father kept a few cows. When David turned 12, he convinced his dad to sell him one of the cows with the money he had saved. Having already learned how the business worked, he saw it as a good investment and wanted to be part of it. The investment slowly began to pay off: one cow became two, and then two became four. Every weekend, David would check on his cows, ensuring they were gaining weight. Although there was significant work behind the scenes and various expenses that had to be covered, his father spared the young cowboy that burden. His dad took care of all the cows, including David's, managing the costs involved in their care, grazing, feeding, and even veterinary visits. For David, his cows were pure profit. Eventually, David realized all this, but in the meantime, he enjoyed the romantic side of the business and the money it generated. He remembers it as an invaluable lesson in investment and responsibility.

By the time David turned 18, he had six cows, which he sold for $600.[37] He was very proud of having achieved that small fortune, a result of his shrewdness and dedication.

David spent a total of 10 years in Costa Rica, a period that was fundamental for his personal and professional development. During that time, he consolidated the skills and values that would define him as a leader. Those years of discipline in Tae Kwon-Do, working in the family factory, and "investments" in the countryside ingrained in him a strong work ethic and entrepreneurial spirit that would accompany him throughout his life.

---

[37] Cfr. Knox, Fortt. Entrevista. Ago 2023. "David Velez, Nubank CEO: A Fortt Knox Conversation".
https://www.youtube.com/watch?v=8ml4yfyut6o

San Francisco

David recalled a conversation he had with his father:

> —*What are you going to be when you grow up?*
> —*What are you going to study?*
> —*I'm going to be a manager,* I said, *thinking that was the best option.*
> —*Or I'm going to start a career in* business *administration.*

But my dad responded:

> —*No, what do you want to manage?*
> —*You're going to be a founder, you're going to start a business, you're going* to build *your own space.*

After finishing high school, David had the opportunity to study at a German university for a year. Fascinated by computers,[38] he began to immerse himself in the study of physics and mathematics. For six or seven months, he dedicated himself enthusiastically to these subjects, convinced that this was his path.

During those years, David was already an avid reader of books about entrepreneurs. The idea of going to Silicon Valley began to consume him, and his mind was constantly occupied with dreams of innovation and technology.

---

[38] Cfr. Fajardo, Sergio. El Profesor. BumBox Podcast. Sep 2023. "Entrevista con David, el banquero que rompió el molde". https://www.youtube.com/watch?v=qqdd6TUZUp4&t=255s

When it came time to decide on his academic future, David knew that the United States was the ideal destination. However, as he applied to the most prestigious universities, he realized he faced a significant disadvantage: he did not have a strong command of English. His strongest languages were Spanish and German, and he was unfamiliar with the intricate admissions processes of American universities, which have their own complexities. To top it off, he did not even know what the SAT was—the famous standardized test for college admission in the United States.

Despite these challenges, David's determination remained steadfast. With the support of his family and his unbreakable spirit of perseverance, he embarked on the arduous task of learning English and understanding the admissions system. His discipline and commitment to his goals led him to quickly improve his language skills and familiarize himself with the requirements of American universities.

David had excelled in high school, graduating with honors, participating in school events, being an athlete, and getting involved in school affairs, even becoming the president of the student association. All of this was topped off with a very good academic average. Undoubtedly, he had excellent credentials to be a candidate for any university.

David sent his admission applications to several universities in the United States. They were all very similar, but he noticed that Stanford's application had a unique feature: a space at the end to write whatever he wanted. So he did. He wrote something like this:

> *Please note that I come from a German school. I haven't learned much English, and I don't know much about the SAT.*
> *I haven't had much help with the admission process.* [39]

Weeks passed, and the universities started to respond to his applications one by one —trickling in with a slowness that is hard for any young person to bear. Each respond was a "no" with message like, *Thank you for applying, you're valuable, but no*. It was terribly disappointing, and quite harsh for any student to endure.

But then one day, a "yes" arrived.

The response was from none other than his dream university, Stanford. He could not believe it; he was ecstatic, bursting with happiness.

Reflecting on the matter, David could not understand why Stanford had said yes. He had applied to all the other universities as a precaution. But the truth was, Stanford was the only university that had captured his interest from day one; Silicon Valley was everything to him.

With no apparent explanation, he had been accepted. Maybe it was that note in his application, the fact that he was a foreigner, his excellent academic record, or perhaps a combination of all three. The fact is, he managed to capture the attention of someone in Stanford's admissions.

---

[39] Cfr. Ididem. Knox, Fortt. Entrevista. Ago 2023.

There was David, with an unerasable smile and a heart racing a mile a minute, thinking that, somehow, magically, his dreams were beginning to come true.

When he arrived at Stanford, his passion for physics and mathematics was still fresh. But suddenly, he found himself in classrooms with Indian, Chinese, and American peers who were literal geniuses in these subjects. He felt completely out of his depth, realizing he was far from being on the same level: *I was never going to be good at this*,[40] he acknowledged humbly. This realization quickly led him to reconsider his academic focus.

Faced with this, he simply "turned the page" and moved on, redirecting his energy and talents toward areas where he could truly stand out and make a difference. With his strong capacity for adaptation, he redefined his goals.

Stanford

David embarked on his adventure in 2001, a time of adjustment and reevaluation in Silicon Valley. Its once-bright allure had faded; it was no longer the legendary hub he had read about and admired. In the late 1990s, Silicon Valley had experienced an unparalleled surge of growth and optimism, largely driven by the rise of dot-com technology companies and the burgeoning popularity of the Internet. Money flowed freely,

---

[40] Caracol Television. Los Informantes TV. Entrevista. Oct. 2023. https://www.facebook.com/CaracolTV/videos/el-colombiano-más-rico-del-mundo-david-David-la-mente-maestra-tras-nubank/863596941744570/

with a massive influx of venture capital fueling tech startups, inflating their valuations, and prompting many to go public with unrealistic expectations.

On March 10, 2000, the NASDAQ index, which included many tech companies, peaked at 5,048 points before plunging dramatically, ultimately losing nearly 78% of its value. This collapse marked the infamous bursting of the dot-com bubble.[41]

Many startups that had received significant investments failed to generate sufficient revenue and began to shut down. Companies like Pets.com and Webvan[42] became emblematic of this debacle. As a result, unemployment in the region soared, with numerous companies either downsizing or closing their doors entirely.

This collapse led to a more cautious approach to evaluating projects. Companies and investors became much more discerning, focusing on sustainable business models and long-term profitability. Despite the crisis, Silicon Valley remained a hub of innovation. Established companies like Apple, Google, and Cisco managed to stay afloat.

---

[41] Sevilla Arias, Andrés. Economipedia. Mar 2020. "Burbuja de las punto-com". https://economipedia.com/definiciones/burbuja-de-las-punto-com.html

[42] Webvan was an e-commerce company founded in 1996 that offered home delivery services for grocery products. Based in Foster City, California, it sought to revolutionize grocery shopping by using the Internet to place orders and ensure fast deliveries. Despite its innovative vision and advanced logistical infrastructure, Webvan faced high operational costs and expanded too quickly, leading to its bankruptcy in 2001. Its story became an iconic example of the dot-com failures of the era.

In the early 2000s, new technologies and trends began to emerge, setting the stage for the next wave of innovation. During this period, the impact of the tech bubble's burst was mitigated by the rise of Apple's smartphones—small yet powerful handheld devices. These phones, with their innovative operating systems and programming languages, enabled the development of efficient and powerful mobile applications. Additionally, the growth of open-source software and the advent of broadband Internet played crucial roles in this technological evolution.

This era was also marked by the birth of social networks and groundbreaking companies. Friendster launched in 2002, followed by LinkedIn and MySpace. SpaceX, founded in 2002, marked the beginning of a new era in private space exploration. Tesla in 2003, Facebook in 2004, and YouTube in 2005.

In this dynamic and challenging environment, David found fertile ground for his personal and professional growth. At Stanford, surrounded by some of the brightest minds in the world, he absorbed knowledge and experiences that would be fundamental.

David enrolled in the Management Science and Engineering (MS&E) program[43] because it was a multidisciplinary field that combined his interests in mathematics, economics, and finance. On one hand, it was an engineering discipline, a science he considered fundamental for solving problems, but it also offered pathways to careers in investment banking, consulting, or product management. With

---

[43] Cfr. Op. Cit. Fajardo, Sergio. El Profesor. BumBox Podcast. Sep 2023. "Entrevista con David".

a balanced mix of business administration and engineering principles, the program provided all the essential tools for aspiring entrepreneurs.

David had a clear purpose: he wanted to start a business and was already immersed in the dynamic world of startups, right in the heart of Silicon Valley. He believed that this was where he would find a promising business idea. Like Diogenes with his lantern, he searched tirelessly, remaining open to any inspiration that might come his way.

However, despite all his efforts and keeping an entirely open mind, he did not discover anything compelling during his first years in the program.

When summer arrived, at 22 years old, it was time to choose a company for an internship. Noticing that many of his friends were heading into finance, he decided to explore that field as well. He joined a traditional financial services company and worked as an Equity Analyst intern at Goldman Sachs in New York City. There, he developed a new interest in financial markets, gained valuable knowledge, and connected with many talented individuals. He stayed with Goldman Sachs until August 2004.

David graduated with an MS&E degree in June 2005.

New York

In 2005, having completed his studies, David found himself still searching for an idea that truly excited him enough to start a business. Despite his efforts, nothing had yet captured his passion. Consequently, he decided to continue advancing his professional career and joined Morgan Stanley to further his financial training. At this prestigious firm, he worked in the investment banking division, managing large financial transactions and advising companies across various sectors. This experience provided him with a solid foundation in corporate finance and banking operations.

A side effect of this job was that it intensified his ambition to become an entrepreneur. During meetings with business owners, he couldn't shake the thought, *I want to be the one on the other side of the table*. After just over two years, he left Morgan Stanley, carrying with him valuable experience and a growing determination to start his own venture.

In July 2007, eager to be even closer to the world of entrepreneurship, he joined General Atlantic,[44] a prestigious venture capital firm. There, he specialized in investments in technology and financial services, allowing him to work closely with real-life entrepreneurs, which he hoped would inspire a new idea.

---

[44] General Atlantic is a global growth equity firm founded in 1980. It specializes in investing in innovative and high-growth companies in sectors such as technology, financial services, healthcare, and consumer. Its strategy is centered on supporting visionary entrepreneurs, providing both capital and operational expertise to drive sustainable growth and global expansion of its portfolio companies. The firm has a strong international presence with offices in North America, Europe, Asia, and Latin America.

Surprisingly and completely unexpectedly, one day, his boss called him in and said:

> *Since you are the person closest to being Brazilian, why don't you go to São Paulo and open an office there?*[45]

It was an intriguing proposal that David accepted with enthusiasm. Within six months, in 2008, he moved from New York to São Paulo, where he embarked on a new and exciting adventure. It was his first time in that vibrant city, and to make things even more challenging, he didn't speak Portuguese.

Brazil

In São Paulo, David started the office from scratch, feeling as though he was already venturing into something entrepreneurial, even if it was under the umbrella of one of the world's largest private equity firms. But, as he thought, something is better than nothing. He quickly fell in love with Brazil, recognizing it as a vast country full of opportunities, but also great challenges.

His role at General Atlantic was exactly what he had hoped for, bringing him very close to entrepreneurs. He frequently met with leaders in sectors as diverse as healthcare,

---

[45] Revista Semana. Semana Noticias. Oct 2022. "Entrevista: habla David, el segundo hombre más rico de Colombia".
https://www.youtube.com/watch?v=RRF8b7jgA4U&t=2319s

commerce, telecommunications, and financial services. There was much to learn, and he eagerly absorbed every opportunity. He participated in board meetings and served on the boards of the companies they financed.

Despite all these opportunities and experiences, David never lost sight of his goal: he wanted to create something of his own, not just work for a company. However, the perfect idea for his venture had not yet materialized.

David often reflected:

> *At General Atlantic, I was sitting across from the entrepreneur. But again, I wanted to be that person; I wanted to be the entrepreneur. I wanted to make the tough decisions—not just advise others, but to do it myself.*

He speculated that the act of learning something new always made him feel alive; discovering new things deeply motivated him. However, he also realized that his motivation waned rapidly once he mastered what he was doing. When the learning stopped and the work became more mechanical, devoid of challenges, he lost interest.

Despite this introspection, the reality was that time continued to pass, and he still hadn't found a concrete idea to pursue. He wasn't meeting his primary objective and began to feel like he was wasting time. The frustration built up, but his determination never wavered; he knew he had to keep searching until he found that spark that would light his own path.

David often found himself thinking:

What am I doing? What is it, ultimately, that I do every day, and where is it leading me? What am I creating?

He realized he needed to take a break, refocus, and search for a potential venture.

But the years continued to pass quietly, without any new ideas. He believed the best way to find inspiration was through studying, concentrating, and reflecting.

At 28, David became increasingly aware that what he truly needed was time alone to reflect. He believed that the best way to achieve this was through a solid business education. It was time for a break—time to return to the classroom, listen, learn, engage in discussions, change his environment, and reconnect with friends. Sometimes, the right thing to do is to take a step back, rest a bit, and unwind by focusing on something constructive.

After three years, David left General Atlantic in June 2010. He returned to California and enrolled in the MBA program at Stanford Graduate School of Business, convinced that this would be the place where he would find the inspiration he had been seeking.

Sequoia Capital

In the fall of 2010, David eagerly began his first quarter, ready to enjoy two years of learning, partying with friends, and moments of reflection.[46]

But destiny had a surprise waiting for him, one that would have a profound impact.

It seems that during his conversations with friends, David would occasionally share his thoughts, desires, and uncertainties. He likely spoke about "doing something" with his classmates, perhaps even asking for ideas or discussing the vast opportunities in Latin America.

At some point that fall, exactly in the third week of his master's program, a classmate named David George approached him and said:

> *David, you need to go find Doug Leone from Sequoia right now. They are looking to investing in Latin America and want to open an office in Brazil.*

David was stunned. Sequoia, the most iconic investment fund in Silicon Valley, was no small player, and Doug Leone was one of its most prominent directors. His curiosity was too strong to resist, so without hesitation, he went

---

[46] Cfr. Stromeyer, Christopher, Interview. Stanford Graduate School of Business. May 2022. Insight by Standford Business. Entrevista con David. https://www.gsb.stanford.edu/insights/david-velez-position-yourself-scarcity-not-oversupply

to seek him out. Sequoia's offices were in West Menlo Park, conveniently close to the university.

Before long, David found himself sitting across from the legendary Doug Leone.[47]

Doug Leone was one of Sequoia's senior directors, responsible for the brand and global operations. Sequoia Capital[48] was known for its extremely flat structure, where directors frequently interacted with one another, and the company had very few hierarchical levels.

David recalls that their conversation was great, though *many unusual things happened during that first meeting*.[49] They talked for about 60 minutes, discussing Brazil, David's work at General Atlantic, as well as his family and personal life. He remembers the conversation as very pleasant, though it felt like an atypical interview for a venture capital firm.

Months later, David realized that the purpose of the interview had been more about assessing his personality than his experience. It had undoubtedly been an in-depth interview—almost a psychological profile. This approach was very much in line with Doug Leone's style, as David came to

---

[47] Douglas M. Leone was born on July 4, 1957, in Italy. He is an American billionaire venture capitalist and former managing partner of Sequoia Capital, a position he left in 2022 while remaining a general partner. As of August 2022, his net worth was estimated at $6.1 billion.
[48] Sequoia Capital is an American venture capital firm based in Menlo Park, California, specializing in seed stage, early stage, and growth stage investments in private companies across all technology sectors. It was founded in 1972. Its principal partners include Michael Moritz, Douglas Leone, Jim Goetz, and Roelof Botha.
[49] Op.Cit., Stromeyer, Christopher, Entrevista. Stanford Graduate School of Business. May 2022.

understand that Leone had an exceptional ability to "read people."

At the end of the interview, Doug simply said:

Come back and meet our people at Sequoia, and let's see what happens.

David recalls leaving Doug Leone's office feeling both puzzled and excited. Just talking to Leone was a significant event, and the possibility of working at Sequoia was something extraordinary. It wasn't just any job—people would do anything to work there. But then there was his master's degree. What would happen to it? Would he have to give up Stanford or turn down the most coveted job offer?

As he reflected on these thoughts, David walked to the parking lot, got into his car, and a minute later, his phone vibrated. He had just received an email. It was from Michael Moritz,[50] another Sequoia director, with a brief message: *Come back. I want to meet you.*

It took Doug Leone less than five minutes to persuade Michael Moritz to interview David on the spot, as though Doug wanted to validate his impressions without any delay. That interview must have been compelling; Moritz, a seasoned interviewer, likely assessed David's personality within minutes.

---

[50] Sir Michael Jonathan Moritz is a venture capitalist, philanthropist, author, and former journalist who was born in Wales and is now a billionaire American. Moritz works at Sequoia Capital and writes the first history of Apple Inc., "The Little Kingdom," as well as "Going for Broke: Lee Iacocca's Battle to Save Chrysler."

Over the next two weeks, David worked on scheduling interviews with the rest of Sequoia's partners. At the end of that period, they extended an offer he could not refuse: to help Sequoia expand into Latin America and explore the possibility of opening an office in Brazil. All of this would be done while David continued his master's program and worked part-time for Sequoia.

The opportunity was invaluable, representing not only an exciting challenge but also a significant validation of his abilities. He felt an immense sense of pride. Sequoia's trust in him to spearhead their entry into such a dynamic market as Latin America was a great honor. Additionally, the arrangement allowed him to continue his studies. Returning to Brazil so soon was something he had never anticipated.

On paper, balancing this new role with his master's studies seemed like a dream come true—surely the envy of his peers. The prospect of blending academic learning with real-world experience was beyond what he could have imagined. Moreover, this role would provide him with a valuable network of contacts and an in-depth understanding of the Latin American market.

Sequoia Capital has been involved from the very beginning with some of the most important startups in history. Among its most iconic investments are companies like Apple, Cisco, Google, Nvidia, Airbnb, Instagram, ServiceNow, YouTube, Stripe, WhatsApp, and many others.

Of course, the idea of starting his own business continued to occupy both his thoughts and his heart. His master's degree was a critical part of his plan, and he did not want to give it up, but the opportunity to work for Sequoia was simply too good to decline. The chance to be in the same room as some of the world's top entrepreneurs, to hear them pitch their ideas, and to learn from them and Sequoia's directors was an extraordinary experience. His goal was to complete his master's while working at Sequoia[51] for the next two years.

As if that were not enough, his office and school were just minutes apart—a convenience he could hardly believe. Yet, it also meant saying goodbye to the two peaceful years of reflection he had once envisioned.

He accepted the offer, but the reality was far from the idealized version one might imagine. It turned out to be too good to be true in some respects; the experience came with a steep price. It was not part-time, nor was it easy. However, without this intense period of learning and growth, Nubank might never have come into being.

This opportunity included working directly with Doug Leone, one of Sequoia's most prominent directors—an unusual situation in the industry. Typically, the youngest associate works with someone at the bottom of the company's hierarchy, not directly with a senior director. But here, the opportunity was even more extraordinary. Not only did he report directly to Leone, but he also had a seat at the board table, where his opinions were valued and heard.

The first time it happened, David's heart nearly stopped. He never imagined they would ask for his opinion, and the worst part was that he had no idea what to say. But he promised

---

[51] Cfr. Stromeyer, Christopher, Interview.

himself that would never happen again. From that day forward, he began preparing "extra business cases" in addition to those required for his master's program. He made sure he was always ready to contribute his thoughts. And when he did, they listened.

During those two years, David balanced his work at Sequoia with his studies. One advantage he had was Brazil being five hours ahead of California, so he would start his day at 4:00 am (9:00 am in Brazil). He spent the first three to four hours making and receiving calls from entrepreneurs in Brazil, scouting for new opportunities. Then, he would return to Stanford for classes from 9:00 am to 2:00 pm. After class, he would head back to Sequoia, usually staying until 6:00 or 7:00 pm, before heading home to tackle his homework.

That so-called "part-time" arrangement was a mere formality. It only meant he was not solely committed to Sequoia because of his academic obligations, but in reality, it was a demanding schedule.

In an interview, David reflected:

> *I lived two lives at once, but it was a wonderful opportunity. I learned so much—being with good friends in the master's program, seeing and experiencing so many new businesses.*[52]

---

[52] Cfr. Stromeyer, Christopher, Entrevista. Stanford Graduate School of Business. May 2022. Insight by Standford Business. Entrevista con David. https://www.gsb.stanford.edu/insights/david-velez-position-yourself-scarcity-not-oversupply

It was true; David was absorbing knowledge from both worlds: the theory he studied at Stanford and the practical experience he gained at Sequoia. He even mentioned that at one point, he asked Sequoia for permission to use some contracts he had worked on as examples in his Investment class to illustrate what was being done in the real world.[53] David even sat on the boards of some of the companies they funded—his experience was as hands-on as it could get.

However, it was also true that both "jobs" were extremely demanding, and it became clear that dedicating 100% to both was impossible. David eventually had to make a choice. In his interview with Cris Stromeyer, Cris asked David:[54]

> *Were they saying you were close to getting the R.J. Miller prize?*
>
> *—No, not at all, not even close. It was impossible; something had to be sacrificed. There is no way you can do everything.*
>
> *It was a real sacrifice. I could not do 100% of the readings; it was just not feasible. I decided to take the risk that a professor might ask me something in class and I would not have an answer, simply because I had not read all*

---

[53] Cfr. Knox, Fortt. Entrevista. Ago 2023. "David Velez, Nubank CEO: A Fortt Knox Conversation"
 https://www.youtube.com/watch?v=8ml4yfyut6o
[54] The R.J. Miller Scholar Award is a recognition given to MBA students who graduate in the top 10% of their class.

the required material. I started to focus only on the most essential 20-30%.

I was embarrassed. I never got used to doing that, but I had to let something go. I could not do it all—I needed to sleep too. And, of course, the prize was what I ended up sacrificing.

In the master's program, there were no classes on Wednesdays, so Tuesday afternoons were usually a time for students to relax and socialize. But not for David. Although there were free days in the academic schedule, his commitments at Sequoia did not allow for much downtime. Additionally, since he had to travel to São Paulo every month or two,[55] he often used those Tuesday afternoons to fly to Brazil for just a single day.

Every week, David balanced his mornings between Sequoia and his master's program. But on some Tuesdays, instead of following his usual routine, he headed to the airport, boarded Doug Leone's private plane, and landed in São Paulo at 8:00 a.m. on Wednesday. Once there, he would have about ten meetings, sign four term sheets, and then return to the airport to fly back to San Francisco. By Thursday morning, he was back in class at Stanford. The flight to São Paulo took nearly 13 hours each way.

David recalls moments on the plane when he would pinch himself, wondering: *Is this real? Am I dreaming? What*

---

[55] Cfr. Leone, Doug. Sequoia. Dec 2021. https://www.sequoiacap.com/article/nubank-ipo-only-the-beginning/

is happening? There were times when the exhaustion caught up with him. Those two years were incredibly intense, and he constantly sought ways to balance everything so it could work.

Doug Leone became his mentor, teaching him invaluable lessons about building and investing in companies. Doug was, after all, the first person to invest in Google when its founders were seeking capital.

David managed to survive this whirlwind experience. In early June 2012, he took his final exams and graduated with his master's degree on June 12.

Phew! Now he could rest a bit... he thought. But no, now the real fun was about to begin.

The Idea

David had been searching for the right business idea for years, but it always eluded him. He had positioned himself in countless ways to discover something promising: he was a student at Stanford University for both his undergraduate and master's degrees, lived in Silicon Valley—the birthplace of thousands of startups and home to countless legends—gained invaluable experience at top-tier companies in the financial and entrepreneurial sectors, and surrounded himself with influential figures in those fields. It seemed like the perfect environment to stumble upon a groundbreaking idea. But no, nothing. No matter how hard he tried, the inspiration never came.

With great patience, he reassured himself that the right opportunity would appear eventually. Hundreds, perhaps thousands, of ideas had crossed his mind, but he dismissed them just as quickly as they appeared. Despite living in the heart of entrepreneurship, no significant opportunity had materialized.

It took 15 years for that moment to arrive. And yes, it finally came—not in Silicon Valley, but in the bustling city of São Paulo, Brazil.

The business opportunity David had been searching for was "complicated" and came with a series of minimum requirements that needed to be met—it wasn't a simple concept.

David once recounted an experience that made him reflect on the kind of company he wanted to create. It couldn't be just any business; it had to be challenging and meaningful.

One thing that became clear to him over time was that it had to be large-scale and based outside the United States.

Before starting his master's program, David attended a conference in New York where several private equity funds from Latin America presented their strategies and pitches. At the end of the event, he felt that all the ideas were essentially the same—nearly clones of concepts already implemented in the U.S.—and none truly addressed the unique challenges of Latin America. This realization connected with a piece of advice Doug Leone had given him: always position yourself on the right side of the market—the side of scarcity, not oversupply.

In the United States, David noticed there was an abundance of talent in the investment sector; the market was crowded with investors, which made Sequoia just one of many firms. But in Latin America, the situation was different. There, he saw a shortage of both talent and capital for entrepreneurship, particularly in the startup space. Companies that could address real local challenges, such as providing better access to banking services, hospitals, and healthcare, were few and far between. The region's weak infrastructure demanded innovative solutions.

These reflections led David to conclude that it made more sense to focus on creating impactful solutions in Latin America, where his experience and knowledge could make a bigger difference. He also considered the potential impact per unit of time invested. He reasoned that it was not worth investing his time in low-impact projects, since they required the same effort as any other venture. Big or small, any meaningful project is hard to execute and can take decades to build. In terms of energy and commitment, the work involved in building something small was not much different from building something big.

During an interview-conference with Stanford MBA students in May 2022, David shared his thoughts on where he believed it was worth dedicating his time and effort. He posed two essential questions to himself:

> —What is the most difficult thing I can imagine doing? What is the most impactful thing I can imagine?
>
> The answer came to him: Banks.
> He explained his reasoning:
>
> In Latin America, the largest companies in Brazil are banks, the largest companies in Mexico are banks, and the largest companies in Argentina are banks. There is nothing bigger. It was the most difficult thing I could imagine and the most impactful because they form an oligopoly.[56]

David had returned to Brazil for the second time with the mission of opening a Sequoia office in the region. He had spent nearly two years working on this effort, investing countless hours connecting with people, interviewing entrepreneurs, and signing and analyzing many potential deals.

---

[56] Cfr. Stromeyer, Christopher, Stanford Graduate School of Business. May 2022. Insight by Standford Business. Entrevista con David Vélez.
https://www.gsb.stanford.edu/insights/david-velez-position-yourself-scarcity-not-oversupply

Yet, despite all this work, no significant breakthroughs had been achieved.

Mariel Reyes Mil

In Brazil, David had a habit of regularly meeting up with a group of friends. As is often the case with such gatherings, new faces would sometimes join, invited by one person or another. One day in 2013, a vibrant and charismatic Peruvian economist from Lima, Mariel Reyes Mil, was introduced to the group. Mariel immediately connected with the group's dynamic and quickly became a regular attendee. It wasn't long before David began to notice her, and soon a spark was lit between them.

They started dating, and as time passed, their relationship grew stronger until they eventually fell deeply in love. Mariel wasn't just captivated by David—she was also drawn to his passion for innovation. So much so that she became one of his earliest supporters and even ended up being Nubank's cardholder number 10. In 2015, they got married, and together they have since built a family with four children.[57]

Mariel has not only been a life partner to David but also a crucial ally in his social efforts. In August 2021, they

---

[57] Caparroso, José. Forbes Colombia. oct 2022. "David Vélez y Mariel Reyes revelan a dónde irán las primeras donaciones de su fortuna" https://forbes.co/2022/10/10/editors-picks/david-velez-y-mariel-reyes-revelan-a-donde-iran-sus-primeras-donaciones

demonstrated their deep commitment to global welfare by signing *The Giving Pledge*,[58] promising to donate $6 billion to charitable causes. Through this act of generosity, they aim to give back to society and share their vision of a better and more just world, establishing a legacy in both business and philanthropy.

Mariel leads the social initiative {REPROGRAMA},[59] part of their philanthropic foundation DavidReyes+,[60] which focuses on reducing inequality in access to opportunities throughout the region. With this initiative, they strive to accelerate social transformation and create more and better

---

[58] In August 2010, 40 of the richest people in the U.S. committed to donating the majority of their wealth to address some of society's most urgent problems. This commitment, known as The Giving Pledge, was created by Warren Buffett, Melinda French Gates, and Bill Gates after a series of conversations with philanthropists about how to establish a new standard of generosity among the ultra-wealthy. It quickly attracted the interest of philanthropists from around the world. It is an open invitation for billionaires to publicly pledge to give away the majority of their wealth to philanthropy either during their lifetimes or in their wills. It aims to change social norms around philanthropy and motivate people to give more, plan their giving earlier, and do so more intelligently. The signatories fund a wide variety of causes of their choice and join a dynamic community of committed philanthropists who share challenges, successes, and ideas to enhance their giving.
https://www.givingpledge.org|https://www.givingpledge.org

[59] {REPROGRAMA} is a social impact initiative whose mission is to reduce racial and gender inequality in technology to promote diversity through education. It offers completely free programming courses for women and teenagers in situations of social, economic, and gender vulnerability, prioritizing Black, trans, and travesti individuals in our selection processes. Additionally, it supports the relocation of its students into the job market and fosters support networks, which are crucial for their continuation in the IT field.

[60] Fundación DavidReyes+. https://velareyesmas.com

opportunities for vulnerable children and young people in Latin America, empowering them to shape their own futures.

Sequoia Leaves Brazil

On October 1, 2012, the phone rang with a tone that signaled bad news. Doug Leone, in his typically blunt manner, delivered the message to David with the precision of a surgeon operating —only without anesthesia:

There won't be a Sequoia office in Brazil.

Doug did not mince words. The reason for this decision was disheartening: the pitches from Brazil's first wave of entrepreneurs had failed to inspire. Their ideas did not meet Sequoia's high standards, leading to the cancellation of the ambitious project.

One statistic proved decisive: the University of São Paulo, Brazil's top institution, had produced only 42 computer science graduates the previous year. It was an alarmingly low number, inadequate to support the kind of tech innovation Sequoia sought to foster. There simply weren't enough engineers in the country. Given this outlook, Doug concluded that the region lacked the necessary technical talent[61] and that the entrepreneurial enthusiasm wasn't backed by groundbreaking ideas. Thus, Sequoia's venture into Brazil came to an end.

David vividly recalled the moment:

---

[61] Cfr. England, Joanna. Banking. FinTech Magazine. Oct. 2022. "Fintech Trailblazer: David, CEO & Co-founder of Nubank".
  https://fintechmagazine.com/banking/fintech-trailblazer

It was a day before my birthday, and it was a shock to me.

Rather than returning to the U.S. defeated, David saw this as a sign that the time had come to launch his own venture. He refused to be discouraged by the news, resigned from Sequoia, and chose to stay in Brazil. Determined to disrupt the financial services industry with a customer-centric approach, he embraced the uncertainty of being jobless and allowed the idea that had been brewing for years to take shape. David began preparing to turn that vision into reality.

The Bank Branch

At one point, turning back the hands of time, David had considered opening a bank account in Brazil to better manage his expenses. So, he made his way to Avenida Brigadeiro Faria Lima, the iconic financial hub of São Paulo, where Brazil's largest banks are headquartered. The avenue was gaining a reputation as the "Brazilian Wall Street" due to the concentration of financial institutions lining its streets.

When David finally found the bank branch he was looking for, he headed toward the entrance. To his dismay, he was met with a double security door—armored, with cameras and metal detectors. He was required to leave his backpack in a locked locker before being allowed inside. As he attempted to enter, the cellphone in his pocket set off the alarms.

Suddenly, the entire branch, including the security guards, turned to stare at him, making him feel as though he were a criminal attempting to rob the bank.

Once the embarrassing ordeal passed, David found himself in a crowded waiting area. It took nearly an hour and a half before he was finally called. When he did get to speak with someone, the interaction was cold and dismissive. The bank employee, showing no sign of interest, bluntly asked, *what do you want? Why are you here?* After David explained his needs, she replied, *you have to fill out this information and bring these documents. When you have everything ready, come back.*

This frustrating and humiliating experience became the catalyst that fueled David's determination to transform the banking landscape in Brazil. He realized there was an immense opportunity to create a bank that truly understood and valued its customers—one that offered friendly, efficient service without the unnecessary complications he had just endured.

David never imagined that what should have been a relatively simple process would turn out to be so complex.[62] It took him over three months to finally open his bank account. He had to return to the branch six or seven times, each time trying to submit the required documents, only to be told that something was missing, incorrectly filled out, or that he now had to go to a different window. The bureaucracy was overwhelming, and the indifference with which he was treated made it worse. He could hardly believe it. There was no effort to treat him as a valued new customer. David couldn't help but

---

[62] Cfr. Op. Cit. Trava, Oswaldo. Podcast. Entrevista "David. Nubank I Cómo ir de $0 a $10 Billones"

think: if this was how they treated him—a professional with extensive training and experience in the financial sector—what chance did the millions of people who had never even dealt with a bank have?

The need became painfully clear: over 250 million Latin Americans lacked access to financial services. Many people still kept their money hidden at home, and when they needed loans, they often turned to predatory lenders who charged them upwards of 500% interest per year—if they were fortunate. The lack of education, particularly financial literacy, left many unable to save or invest their money effectively.

The need was unmistakable: over 250 million Latin American consumers had no access to financial services. These people often stored their money under the mattress, and when they needed loans, they turned to loan sharks who charged them no less than 800% interest annually—if they were lucky. The lack of education, particularly financial literacy, left many without the knowledge of how to save or invest effectively.

That painful truth, as expressed by Dan Schulman, President and CEO of PayPal: *The less you have, the more you pay* [63] —is a brutal reality for millions.

Amid his frustration, after countless trips back and forth to the bank, gathering documents, and filling out forms, David began to see the immense opportunity in front of him. The pain, the dissatisfaction, and the frustration with banking services were undeniable. The banks, an oligopoly, had no incentive to

---

[63] FII Institute. Jun 2024. "David Vélez Analyzes Brazil's Domination in #fintech" https://www.youtube.com/watch?v=gFo5npXxOgY

change. They operated in the same way they always had, perpetuating an outdated and exclusionary system.

David recognized that the opportunity lay in this vast space for innovation and improvement in financial services—making them accessible, fair, and customer-centric. This vision would soon become the foundation of Nubank, a bank built to empower consumers and treat them with the dignity and respect they deserved. His mission was to educate and support millions of people who had been excluded from the traditional banking system, ultimately revolutionizing the financial sector and making a lasting impact.

In the end, David finally got the bank account he had requested. However, upon reviewing it, he saw clearly the sharp "nails" that inflicted so much pain on consumers—the exorbitant fees and unfair conditions. The account came with a monthly fee of nearly $100 USD for the supposed "privilege" of having it. To add insult to injury, the bank had generously provided him with a credit card that carried an astonishing 500% annual interest rate.

This experience only strengthened David's resolve. The exploitation of consumers by the banking system was immense, and it was clear that change was not just needed—it was urgent.

Traditional Banking

Banking systems around the world tend to follow a similar structure, particularly when it comes to credit risk management, which is nearly identical across different markets. Their basic premise is to set interest rates on loans and credit cards based on the likelihood of default and non-payment. In systems like Brazil's, where defaults and non-payments are common, those who do pay are punished by high interest rates—essentially covering the losses caused by those who don't.[64]

Despite being highly profitable for banks, the institutions behave as though they are doing their customers a favor. The banking system is rarely customer-focused; instead, it prioritizes maintaining its own structure and maximizing profits. This leaves consumers at a disadvantage, treated more like a nuisance than valued clients.

As David considered how he could make the greatest impact, he recognized that banks, as the largest companies in Latin America, operated like an oligopoly that negatively affected the population. The solution? Create real competition—a daunting challenge in such a powerful sector, but one that promised enormous impact.

David knew that even a small improvement in the banking industry could create a ripple effect across the region, benefiting countless people. If traditional banks felt threatened, they might finally awaken from their complacency and start paying attention to their customers to keep them from leaving.

---

[64] Cfr. CB Insight. The Economist. Jun 2018. An Interview with David Vélez, Nubank and Vijay Vaitheeswaran.
https://www.youtube.com/watch?v=VdO2rJCjfzc

This is exactly what happened. Today, many traditional banks have taken significant steps to avoid being left behind. But it wasn't because of their own initiative—it was because of the pressure created by innovative challengers like Nubank.

To bring his venture to life, David had been quietly accumulating a series of strategic advantages over the years — a great number of aces up his sleeve for years. Now, it was time to start shaping that long-desired idea. With his deep background in the financial sector, he was fluent in the industry's jargon. He was in a country where competition for his idea would be minimal, at least in the beginning.

David threw himself into developing his idea, dedicating eight intense weeks to fully explore the opportunity.[65] He read and studied voraciously—books on banking, technology, and the history of financial institutions. He performed a thorough analysis from multiple angles.[66] His brainstorming led him to consider not just one idea, but four or five different industries that intrigued him. However, his frustrating experience opening a bank account in Brazil ultimately guided his direction.

He began talking with bankers and ex-bankers in Brazil, having 20 to 30 coffee meetings where he asked why they weren't competing with each other. Their answers were revealing. They all agreed that modernizing banking in Brazil was impossible. They cited the country's poor internet infrastructure, customers' lack of proper devices, and

---

[65] Cfr. Op. Cit. Fajardo, Sergio. El Profesor. BumBox Podcast. Sep 2023. "Entrevista con David"
[66] Cfr. Op. Cit. Trava, Oswaldo. Podcast. Entrevista "David. Nubank I Cómo ir de $0 a $10 Billones"

widespread distrust of new systems. They also mentioned that Unibanco bank had already tried a similar initiative back in 1999 and had failed.

In these conversations, David sought to align his ideas with reality. Thanks to his previous roles, he was able to speak directly with presidents and former presidents of banks, gathering their insights and opinions—not just from Brazil, but from other Latin American countries as well. These discussions helped him refine his vision. Though the challenge was formidable, it became increasingly clear that the opportunity to revolutionize banking in the region was even more significant.

At the end of these conversations, he always asked the key question:

What do you think about a 100% digital bank, without branches?

David asked, time and again. The response was almost unanimous:

That will never work. People don't trust it, the regulator won't allow it, especially because you're a foreigner. People want a physical branch—that's what gives them confidence.

It was hard to refute these opinions, as they reflected the deeply ingrained mindset of traditional banking. It seemed that the industry had convinced itself that banking had always been done a certain way and should continue to follow that model. There were decades of experience backing this belief. But David saw this as an opportunity—to challenge the status quo and prove that a 100% digital bank was not only possible but necessary for the future of financial services in Latin America.

David became increasingly excited and motivated by the challenge. The difficulty of the task only encouraged him further, but what drove him most was his desire to make a significant impact in the sector and in the region.

He adopted a mentality of focusing his energy on the most significant challenges. If he was going to build a business, why not tackle the biggest and most difficult obstacles? Why invest the same effort into something with less impact when he could aim higher? This mindset led David to fully embrace the idea that a 100% digital bank could revolutionize the banking industry in Brazil and beyond, offering accessible and fair services to millions of people who had been left behind by traditional banks.

At the time, the five largest banks in Brazil (Itaú, Bradesco, Santander, Banco do Brasil, and Caixa) controlled 80% of the market. They were making enormous profits through high interest rates and excessive fees while providing terrible customer service. A Brazilian friend bluntly told David, *Brazilian banks suck. They've always been like that and always will be.*

In one interview, David recalled:

> *There were gigantic opportunities to disrupt industries like banking that no one was really analyzing because no one thought it was possible.*

David also recognized that Nubank might never have been started by a local entrepreneur. It needed someone from Silicon Valley who could see the story of the little ant fighting the elephant and actually winning. *A Latin American investor hears that and is going to tell you: no way, the elephant is going to crush you.* [67]

The Banking Model Can Change

David delved into the study of emerging digital banks, such as Capital One in the United States, which had intrigued him since his time at General Atlantic. He was particularly interested in how these banks efficiently used data analysis. He also explored ING Direct's[68] success in Europe and even traveled to Russia to meet with executives from Tinkoff Bank,[69]

---

[67] Cfr. Kauflin, Jeff. Forbes. Abr 2021

[68] ING Direct is a subsidiary of the Dutch banking group ING Group, known for being a pioneer in direct and digital banking, offering financial services via the Internet and mobile phones. Founded in 1997, ING Direct focused on providing savings accounts, mortgages, and investment products without fees and with competitive interest rates. The entity is recognized for its innovative approach to reducing operational costs by eliminating the need for physical branches and providing customer service through digital platforms.

[69] Tinkoff Bank, today T-Bank, formerly known as Tinkoff Credit Systems, is a Russian commercial bank headquartered in Moscow. It was founded in 2006 by Oleg Tinkov as a digital bank, without branches or physical offices, making it part of the so-called neobanks.
https://es.wikipedia.org/wiki/Tinkoff_Bank

a digital bank with a model similar to Capital One's, which had also achieved significant success.

David's initiative with Nubank would begin with credit cards and gradually expand into other financial services, all while leveraging technology to cut operational costs. This, in turn, would allow Nubank to undercut the exorbitant fees charged by traditional banks, offering greater convenience and more customer-friendly services.

The entrenched banking industry in Brazil had built a perception that they were untouchable, protected by the Central Bank and supported by the country's most powerful families. But for David, as a foreigner with a fresh perspective and a certain amount of naivety, he saw precisely this environment as an opportunity, regardless of the complexity. He believed Nubank could challenge this status quo, providing a modern and fair alternative for millions of Brazilians.

In his exploratory interviews, many bankers had expressed concerns about Brazil's poor internet infrastructure. But the reality told a different story: Brazil ranked in the global top five in usage of social platforms like Instagram, Facebook, and YouTube. The bankers were unaware of this, failing to see the potential that the digital landscape offered.

Technology was the game-changer. In 1999, competing with the big banks would have required a billion dollars just to open branches on every corner and maintain massive data centers. But by 2012, the landscape had shifted dramatically. The rise of smartphones had torn down those barriers, making it possible to reach 100% of the population. That was where the true opportunity lay.

David felt ready. He had the experience and believed he could easily secure financing, knowing the world of venture capital better than most. He had worked with and was well-acquainted with the directors of Sequoia Capital, the most prestigious venture capital firm in the world. He knew their motto: *We help the daring build legendary companies. From idea to IPO and beyond.*[70] Sequoia had seen the boldest ideas in entrepreneurship, and David was confident that his proposal wouldn't intimidate them.

With this in mind, David decided the time had come. He was going to create a bank—a digital bank built from the ground up.

Surprisingly, the enormity of the idea didn't faze him. He viewed the challenge with remarkable candor, believing that such an adventure wasn't as daunting as it might appear. He was completely convinced of the urgent need for change in Brazil's banking sector, and that conviction alone fueled him. There wasn't a single person he spoke to who was satisfied with their banking experience. Every conversation brought up new horror stories about the abysmal service customers received. And yet, no one doubted that the banking industry was an incredibly profitable business.

David decided to take a few days to reflect and further refine his vision, so he took the opportunity to visit his parents. During a car ride, he casually shared his idea with his father. As they drove down the road, his father was caught off guard and

---

[70] Sequoia. Our Ethos. "We help the daring build legendary companies".
https://www.sequoiacap.com/our-ethos/

thought he hadn't fully grasped what David was saying. He slowed the car, pulled over to the side of the road, and looked him straight in the eye, asking directly:

> *You're going to start a bank?*
> *—And in Portuguese?*

David nodded, passionately laying out his vision of a 100% digital bank that would transform the banking industry in Brazil. His father, though surprised, could see the fire of determination in his son's eyes. He knew David well and had watched him achieve so much already. There was no doubt that David was committed to seeing this ambitious venture through, setting the stage for what would become an adventure that would forever reshape the financial landscape in Latin America.

From October to December 2012, David spent time traveling back and forth between Brazil and Colombia, refining his idea and determining the best way to present it to potential investors. Each trip helped him mature his concept, gain a deeper understanding of the market, and develop a plan that would persuade investors of the revolutionary potential of his project.

The Pitch Deck

With his idea polished and fully developed, including the company's name, "EOS," David was eager to register his future venture. However, he was met with disappointment when he discovered the name was already taken. Undeterred, he swiftly pivoted, renaming the company "EO2," a name that closely resembled the original. With the paperwork in hand, David waved his flag—the revolution had begun!

Driven by the determination of an alchemist turning dreams into reality, David crafted a Pitch Deck consisting of 13 meticulously designed PowerPoint slides.[71] In this deck, still using the name EOS, he presented his bold vision of a company that would revolutionize the financial services industry.

Each slide was carefully constructed to capture the attention of investors. Drawing on his experience at Sequoia, David emphasized the key points that would make EOS a force to be reckoned with in the market. With a potent combination of data, analysis, and a compelling narrative, he was ready to share his vision and secure the backing needed to bring EOS to life.

EOS: The Future of Brazilian Consumer Banking.

David's pitch was methodical and direct, though it might have appeared too simple for such a complex and ambitious project. Slide number 4 encapsulated his vision most vividly: a color drawing of the biblical scene from 1 Samuel, chapter 17, where the young David, armed with only a sling and five smooth stones, faces the mighty Philistine giant, Goliath. The image powerfully symbolized David's mission— the established banks were the Goliaths, the fearsome giants,

---

[71] Original Pitch Deck of EOS, Before It Became Nubank. https://www.slideshare.net/PedroRagazzoPaiva/nubank-pitch-deckfinalpdf

and he, like his biblical namesake, would challenge them with a single, well-aimed stone.

    By March 2013, David was preparing to launch his first round of financing, seeking seed capital to bring his venture to life. He returned to Sequoia's offices in Menlo Park, San Francisco, determined to pitch his idea to his former mentor and boss, Doug Leone. Armed with the belief that his strong relationship with Doug and the transformative potential of his project would carry the day, David prepared to face his own Goliath—ready to sell his vision and begin the journey to transform Brazil's financial landscape.

EOS

VISA

EOS - THE FUTURE OF BRAZILIAN CONSUMER BANKING

David's idea was indeed revolutionary: he envisioned a tech company with a fresh, young, and defiantly countercurrent culture. This would be a simple yet powerful company, built around a 100% consumer-focused approach. In short, it would be the Anti-bank!

EOS aimed to construct a digital bank in Brazil that would radically upend the traditional banking model. In a landscape where Brazilian banks were entrenched in an outdated, customer-averse culture of complexity, EOS saw a golden opportunity. Its vision was to attract young, tech-savvy consumers by offering them straightforward, personalized financial products through digital channels—both online and mobile.

EOS would be more than just different; it would be agile. By harnessing data and analytics, it would develop personalized credit products, adopting a process of rapid testing and iterative improvement. This strategy would allow EOS to outpace the big banks, swiftly adapting to changing consumer preferences and technological advances in Brazil. David was confident that with this approach, EOS wouldn't just compete with the banking giants—it would surpass them, transforming the banking experience into something truly customer-centric.

Fueled by his conviction that his proposal could reshape the financial landscape, David presented his vision with unwavering passion and determination. He believed that his disruptive approach would resonate with investors, ultimately securing the backing necessary to make it a reality.

David proposed that Sequoia participate in the seed funding with an investment of $2 million.

ORIGINS OF NUBANK

Here are some key sequences from the **Pitch Deck that David Vélez crafted:**

Brazilian Banks Today

	"Bank"	"Technology company"
Ethos:		
Culture:	Inertia; leverages complexity to confound	New, young, contrarian; leverages simplicity to create **loyalty**
Distribution:	Offline (branches)	Online (online, mobile, **telephone**)
Focus:	Process	Customer experience
Product portfolio:	"One size fits all"	"Right product to the right person at the right price"
Market:	Everybody, everywhere	Smart, technology-savvy consumer
Organization:	Bureaucratic, Hierarchical, rigid	Lean, flat, fast-iteration, agile
IT organization:	12 - 24 months development cycles; 2-3 new products per year	12 - 24 days development cycles; 2-3 new products tested **per day**

Capture the hearts of the consumer

"Brain" = Analytical backbone	"Heart" = Emotional appeal
➤ Data-driven culture of a *technology company, not a bank* ➤ Sophisticated credit analytics; real proprietary underwriting ➤ Full product customization ➤ Fast product introduction and iteration; continuous testing ➤ Complete integration of Credit/IT/Operations/Marketing ➤ *De-novo* architecture built for flexibility, scalability and speed	➤ Brand *"is young, contrarian, breaks with the status-quo, and starts a revolution"* ➤ Completely customer-centered ➤ Simple and intuitive product design ➤ Complete transparency; no "hidden fees" ➤ Internet and mobile channels drive convenience, loyalty

Unique confluence of factors opening a crack in the armor

Macro shifts	Technology shifts	Consumer tastes shift
- Consumer interest-rate sensitive for first time (lowest interest rate environment ever) - Highest concentration of banks ever (internal complexity is paralyzing) - Big banks looking inwards - Government is an ally	- Internet/mobile decrease largest barrier to entry (capital) - Explosion of data commoditizes internal banks data - Beginning of "virtualization of cash" - Cloud-computing/big-data increase underwriting power	- 50% of Brazilians are under 29yrs - Enough trust on the online channel to transact (ecommerce now a $24bn mkt.) - By 2015, there will be 80mm people with mobile internet access - Brazil: "The Social Media Capital of the Universe" (WSJ) - Consumers→ control

Business Model

- Appropriate pricing will be a discovery process; initially we don't plan to compete on price:

Revenue source	Type	% of Portfolio	Price
Interest income	Installment loan	70 – 80%	0%
Interest income	Revolving loan	10% - 20%	8% (month)
Fee	Initialization Fee	-	R$100 – R$300 (once)
Fee	Maintenance Fee	-	R$100 – R$300 (yearly)
Fee	Interchange from merchant	-	~1%

- However, there might be an opportunity to disrupt by changing pricing structure (ie. lowering revolving rate)

Main Risk

- 60 – 80% of credit card transactions are for interest-free installment payments
- "Base case" scenario we operate with similar portfolio of credit card loans (60 – 80% installments)
- "Upside case" we decrease interest rates on revolving, providing incentive for consumers to revolve (as customers globally do)

> **Inception**
>
> **Raising $2mm seed investment**
> - Recruit core engineering team
> - Develop front-end product
> - Design back-end architecture
> - Develop three initial credit models and customer acquisition strategy for each
> - Set-up legal and securitization structure, and close partnership with bank

Slide 1: Introduction
EOS, the future of Brazilian consumer banking.

Slide 2: The Problem
Traditional Brazilian banks are complex, customer-unfriendly, and expensive. They offer poor customer service and charge exorbitant fees.

Slide 3: The Opportunity
Brazil is a growing market with over 250 million consumers, many of whom are dissatisfied with their current banking options. There is a significant demand for a customer-centric, digital banking solution.

Slide 4: The Solution
EOS: A 100% digital bank that prioritizes the customer. Simple, transparent, and efficient. EOS will offer personalized financial products tailored to individual needs.

Slide 5: Market Strategy
Target young, tech-savvy consumers through online and mobile channels. Utilize data and analytics to constantly refine and improve product offerings. Rapidly test and integrate new features based on customer feedback.

Slide 6: Competitive Advantage
EOS will leverage technology to keep operating costs low, allowing us to offer better rates and lower fees than traditional banks. Our agile approach will enable us to stay ahead of market trends and consumer demands.

Slide 7: Financial Projections
Projected growth over the next five years:
- Year 1: 100,000 customers
- Year 2: 500,000 customers
- Year 3: 1 million customers
- Year 4: 2 million customers
- Year 5: 5 million customers

Slide 8: The Team
David Vélez, Founder & CEO - Experienced in financial markets and venture capital.
Key hires from leading tech companies and financial institutions.

Slide 9: Technology Infrastructure
State-of-the-art digital platform. Secure, scalable, and designed for rapid innovation. Built to handle millions of transactions seamlessly.

Slide 10: Milestones and Timeline
Q1 2013: Secure seed funding
Q2 2013: Develop MVP (Minimum Viable Product)
Q4 2013: Launch beta version
Q1 2014: Public launch
Q3 2014: Reach 100,000 customers

Slide 11: Funding Requirements
To bring this vision to life, we are seeking $2 million in seed capital. These funds will be used for:
- Technology development
- Initial marketing and customer acquisition
- Regulatory compliance and licensing
- Team expansion.

Slide 12: Why Sequoia?
Sequoia's track record of supporting disruptive ventures aligns perfectly with our vision. Together, we can revolutionize the Brazilian banking industry.

Slide 13: Conclusion
Join us in creating the future of banking in Brazil. EOS is not just a bank; it's a movement towards a better, fairer financial system for everyone.

Doug Leone was not thrilled with David's idea.

> *It's interesting, but it's something Sequoia would never do. We don't know anything about banks, you know we don't make initial investments in Brazil, and we don't understand anything about credit cards. It doesn't make any sense to us,* he told him.

Maybe he noticed David's disappointment because he added in a more personal tone:

> *But I would invest my own money in you. You did well at Sequoia, and I'd like to help you.*[72]

On a roll, and with his characteristic frankness, Doug Leone didn't hesitate to remind David of all the challenges ahead. He pointed out that David had no experience in commercial banking and proceeded to list several "no's," highlighting the considerable gaps in David's background. Doug emphasized the steep obstacles that would stand in the way of such an ambitious venture.

> *"You don't know banks, you have no retail banking experience, and you don't understand credit cards. You're not Brazilian; you're a complete foreigner who barely knows Brazilians. You don't know the regulators, you have no connections, and you have no way to*

---

[72] Cfr. Trava, Oswaldo (Oso). #065 David. "Nubank, Cómo ir de $0 a $10 billones" https://www.youtube.com/watch?v=DUSHmeEGkoQ

raise capital in Brazil. What Brazilian would even dare compete against the country's lifelong banks?"

The picture Doug Leone painted was undeniably discouraging. And the truth was, he wasn't wrong; every Brazilian investor David had approached had rejected the idea. They found it too risky, with some even reacting in near panic to his proposal: *...they are going to crush you like a cockroach.*[73]

But David was not willing to give up. He remained convinced that his vision of creating a consumer-focused bank in Brazil was solid, and he was determined to find a way to turn it into a reality.

Strategic Adjustments

The truth was, David didn't take kindly to being called inexperienced. Despite his impressive resumé, strong background in private equity, and a master's degree from Stanford, Doug's criticism stung deeply. However, David recognized that Doug was right. Instead of feeling defeated, he chose not to back down.

Inspired by the conversation with Doug, David made strategic adjustments to his pitch. With Doug's approval, he presented the revised version to the other Sequoia directors over a two-week period. Slowly but surely, he managed to shift

---

[73] Cfr. Chu, Michael, et al. Harvard Business School. Caso 9-321-068. Rev. Ago 2023. "Nubank: Democratizing Financial Services"

their perspectives and eventually convinced them that his idea had real potential.

David appealed to the essence of Sequoia, reminding them of what the firm had always done—backing small startups that dared to take on industry giants. He pointed out how Sequoia had invested the first million dollars in Steve Jobs to help create Apple and challenge IBM.[74] They had supported Airbnb against the hotel industry, Google, Kayak, LinkedIn, Nvidia—the list went on. These were the timeless battles of Davids against Goliaths, and that fighting spirit was part of Sequoia's DNA. Now, the battleground was the Brazilian banking industry. Wasn't this exactly the kind of bold venture they had always championed? Wasn't it a good idea?

With this narrative, David managed to get the Sequoia directors to see the potential of his project. Supporting EOS would be another chapter in Sequoia's tradition of betting on daring innovators who sought to disrupt the status quo.

The First Investor

The intensive use of technology was the key reason Sequoia saw a viable opportunity in David's idea. The ability to digitize processes and products, reducing operational costs while offering more efficient and customer-centric services, was at the heart of EOS's proposal. David emphasized how advances in technology could overcome the traditional barriers that had kept Brazilian banking stagnant and uncompetitive.

---

[74] Cfr. Op. Cit. Trava, Oswaldo #065

Doug Leone reflected on their early support:

> *(...) in those early days, Nubank was little more than an idea. Our decision to partner with seed capital was largely based on the person of David Vélez. Yes, we shared his enthusiasm for building not just a credit card company, but a technology company with a consumer-obsessed culture that offered a wide range of online financial services, especially for the relatively young population of Latin America.*[75]

Sequoia agreed to back David's venture, but they set specific conditions, to give him 50% of the seed capital, they proposed:

> *We will contribute 1 million dollars, but you must secure the other million locally or in the region.*
>
> *You need a Brazilian co-founder who knows banking and has relevant contacts in the region.*
>
> *You also need to get a great technology expert to be your CTO and build the applications.*

---

[75] Cfr. Leone, Doug. Sequoia. Dec 2021.
https://www.sequoiacap.com/article/nubank-ipo-only-the-beginning/

Doug Leone also advised David to change the company's name from EOS, which he found *horrible, too nerdy*, suggesting he work with a local agency to find a better name and develop a cohesive brand. Taking this advice to heart, David enlisted a Brazilian branding company. From their proposals, he was drawn to the name "NU," which in Portuguese means *bare, naked, nothing to hide, simple and transparent*. The name also evoked the idea of something "new," aligning with David's vision for a modern, transparent bank. Thus, Nubank was born, along with its distinctive bright purple branding.

Securing the second million proved harder than David had anticipated, even with Sequoia's backing. He contacted no fewer than 30 investors, and 29 turned him down. It became clear that he would not be able to secure funding from any Brazilian investors at this stage.

The investment fund that said yes was Kaszek Ventures,[76] based in Argentina. David knew them well, particularly due to their involvement with Mercado Libre. Two of Kaszek's founders were also Stanford MBA graduates, which, combined with Sequoia's backing, helped open the door to a smooth conversation. Within two weeks, David successfully secured the second million dollars.

---

[76] KASZEK Ventures es una de las firmas de capital de riesgo más grandes de América Latina, fundada por los ex ejecutivos de Mercado Libre. Los fundadores de Mercado Libre son Marcos Galperin y Hernán Kazah. Marcos Galperin es el CEO de Mercado Libre, mientras que Hernán Kazah es uno de los socios de KASZEK Ventures.

By March 2013, David had secured his initial capital. His top priority then became assembling a team to bring his project to life. Taking Sequoia's advice to heart, he focused on addressing his business's key gaps:[77] finding someone with retail banking knowledge and strong connections in Brazil, and a technology expert who could establish the company's technological foundation.

After interviewing more than 60 candidates, David found his second co-founder, Cristina Junqueira, a Brazilian with deep banking experience. She had recently served as the director of credit cards at Banco Itaú and had numerous contacts within the Brazilian financial industry. Cristina was thrilled by the idea and immediately accepted.

For the technology side, Bill Coughran, a partner at Sequoia and former Senior VP of Engineering at Google, recommended Edward Wible, who had worked at Francisco Partners. After David met with Edward in Argentina, Edward became enthusiastic about the project and arrived in São Paulo a week later with just a small suitcase and a backpack, ready to work. He became the third co-founder.

With Cristina's banking expertise and Edward's technological know-how, the founding team of Nubank was complete, and they were ready to launch their purple revolution in the Brazilian banking industry.

---

[77] Cfr. Morris, Nigel. Interview with David. Fintech Nexus. Jun 2022.

Foundation of Nubank

Thus, on May 6, 2013,[78] a Brazilian, an American, and a Colombian officially founded Nubank in São Paulo, Brazil.

However, the process of formalizing the company was anything but smooth. What should have been routine tasks became complex and time-consuming. It took nearly six months to get everything in order—incorporating the company, registering in various places, and even opening a bank account to receive their initial investment. Bringing in the seed capital David had secured proved to be far more complicated than expected, requiring extensive paperwork and legal navigation.

In the meantime, the founders pooled whatever personal funds they had to keep the project moving while they waited for the investment money to come through. Cristina recalled the challenges:

> *Opening an account in most banks was not possible. They wouldn't open an account for such a young company; you had to be established for at least two years. Of course, you wonder, how can you survive those first two years if you can't get a bank account beforehand? There were many obstacles to overcome from day one.*[79]

---

[78] NU, Blog. "NU cumple 10 años de desafiar el sistema financiero". https://blog.NU.com.mx/NU-cumple-10-anos.
[79] Cfr. Novak, Turner. The Peel. Entrevista. Jan 2024. "Building Nubank, The World's Largest Neobank with Co-founder Cristina Junqueira". https://www.youtube.com/watch?v=kUP17aGbY3Y

These challenges only underscored the need for the very revolution Nubank was seeking to bring to the banking industry.

The House on Rua California

Although they had the funds to rent modest offices in a corporate building, the founders decided to rent a small house to keep costs low and avoid surprises. After viewing several properties, they settled on an old two-story house at 492 Rua California, in the Brooklyn neighborhood of São Paulo. This house would serve as Nubank's headquarters for its first few years.

The second floor was perfect for Edward Wible, who moved in there to live with his dog. Soon after, a programmer also moved in and lived there for a while.

The second floor became a home for Edward Wible, who moved in with his dog, and later a programmer also moved in temporarily. The address, Rua California, delighted the founders as it subtly connected them to San Francisco. They paid $500 USD per month for the house, which was just over 100 square meters. With 12 people—9 employees and the 3 founders—working there, the small space felt tight. Michael Abramson, a partner at Sequoia, was impressed by the low cost of the headquarters, unaware that 20 more people were working remotely from their homes. At first, there were no chairs, and many employees had to work on the floor. Furniture arrived gradually, much of it donated through Cristina's efforts.

Despite the humble setup, there was excitement among the team about building the largest financial institution in Latin America, even if it didn't seem like it at the time.

Hiring programmers, however, proved difficult. David and Edward thought offering a 20% higher salary than market rates would attract candidates, but 9 out of 10 prospects turned away after seeing the house. *That was not the office a financial institution should have*, they were told, as it failed to inspire confidence. David recalled watching from the window as candidates approached the house, saw it, and promptly walked away.

Unintentionally, the house became *the perfect interview filter*. The second filter was the project itself: after hearing the details of what they intended to build—a new bank—many candidates lost interest, deeming the venture too complicated or even impossible.

Meanwhile, the programmers and founders were fully immersed in creating Nubank's first product. They worked intensely, designing and coding to bring the first MVP (minimum viable product) of the credit card to life.

Interestingly, what they had anticipated to be difficult ended up being easier than expected. People had repeatedly warned David that regulatory approval would be a major obstacle, but to their surprise, the process turned out to be more accessible than they imagined. Some regulators even expressed enthusiasm for Nubank's proposal; they were not happy with the fact that Brazil's five largest banks controlled 90% of the market and welcomed the idea of competition.

Although regulators supported the innovation Nubank brought to the market, they made it clear that they would not relax any legal requirements. They encouraged the team to comply fully with all regulations, even offering assistance in navigating them, as they wanted to see the fintech sector flourish in Brazil.

This unexpected openness from the regulatory authorities was a major boost for Nubank, providing a bit of sweet relief amidst all the challenges. With the regulators' conditional approval and support, Nubank could move forward with greater confidence, reinforcing the founders' belief that they were on the right path to creating a modern and viable alternative to traditional banks.

Nubank stayed in the house on Rua California for two years, eventually outgrowing the space with nearly 25 people working there, many of them on the floor. They moved to another house before finally, in November 2022, securing more suitable and dignified offices.

Today, Nubank occupies an 8-story building in the heart of one of São Paulo's busiest commercial areas, at the corner of R. Capote Valente and Av. Rebouças in Pinheiros. The nearly cubic building, once a former commercial space, has been completely renovated, featuring a striking exterior of purple and gray panels. Inside, every floor is filled with thousands of elements reflecting Nubank's unique culture.

The lobby is an inviting open space for visitors, offering free WiFi, a café, and a playful violet-colored ball pit, which has become a popular spot for relaxing, working, and snapping photos.[80]

The Credit Card

Nubank's first product to hit the market was a revolutionary credit card, boldly designed in the most striking color they could choose: purple. David and his dedicated team faced the daunting challenge of navigating the complex and stringent requirements set by Brazilian regulators to gain authorization as a Payment Institution (*Instituição de Pagamento*)[81]. They had to build everything from the ground up, despite having little prior experience.). They did everything from scratch, without really having any prior experience.

This process involved not only a deep dive into the legal regulations and procedures but also the creation of the technology needed to ensure their credit card met all legal standards while delivering an outstanding user experience.

The card had to be more than just functional; it needed to offer an intuitive app that allowed users to easily manage

---

[80] Nubank. Editorial. Ene 2023. "Get to know Nubank's main headquarters in Pinheiros, Sao Paulo/Brazil" https://building.nubank.com.br/nubank-office-pinheiros/
[81] Banco Central de Brasil. Instituciones de Pago.
https://www.bcb.gov.br/estabilidadefinanceira/instituicaopagamento

their expenses, pay bills, and access real-time customer support—all from their mobile devices. Building a strong, reliable infrastructure for support, control, and connectivity was essential to guarantee efficient and seamless service. The idea was that customers should not miss the traditional bank branch; everything had to be accessible directly from their phones. Their ambitious goal was to reach one million customers in five years[82]—a target that seemed nearly impossible at the time. Yet, they achieved that milestone in less than two years, despite numerous obstacles along the way.

Several critical decisions and agreements shaped the process, one of the most significant being the choice of which card network to partner with: MasterCard or Visa. Cristina Junqueira's connections from her previous role as a credit card executive at Itaú proved invaluable in paving the way for that crucial decision.

The Purple Card

The card was designed to be remarkably easy to acquire. The process would be so simple that it required only four basic criteria: the applicant had to be of legal age, reside in Brazil, be registered in the Brazilian tax system, and own a smartphone. As long as these requirements were met, anyone could get a card within minutes and have it delivered to their home within two to three days. This was a stark contrast to the

---

[82] Morris, Nigel. Entrevista con David. Fintech Nexus. Jun 2022. "How this Digital Bank Brought Millions of People into the Financial System, Nubank (Full Session)" https://www.youtube.com/watch?v=yXLWiqPEt6U

lengthy paperwork, signatures, and the eight-week wait typically required by traditional banks.

Nubank would determine the credit limit using a sophisticated risk assessment system they planned to build from the ground up. Initially, however, they would use a generic application available on the market, along with consultations with credit bureaus and additional creative parameters to evaluate the risk of each applicant.

While the physical card would be delivered to the customer's doorstep within a few days, they could start using the digital version immediately, as it would be instantly enabled on their phone. An appealing feature was the promise of automatic credit line increases for responsible usage. It was designed to be as easy as possible—"almost" effortless.

Payment Processing

The negotiation with the card processors, which initially seemed like a mere formality, quickly turned into an unexpected and nerve-wracking ordeal. In a stunning blow to their expectations, Visa outright rejected Nubank's proposal, stating they had no interest in working with fintech companies. This setback heightened the tension, leaving all hopes pinned on MasterCard. Another rejection would mean the premature end of their ambitious financial venture.

Thankfully, MasterCard agreed to the partnership. However, they required specialized computing equipment for card processing—equipment that could not be procured in time due to an unforeseen import delay. Without this equipment on hand, Nubank had to find a partner bank that already possessed it in order to meet MasterCard's processing requirements. Though this condition was a significant hurdle, the team remained undeterred, ready to knock on the doors of various banks to secure what they needed.

But instead of just one or two banks, they had to visit fifteen. Each one rejected their proposal, showing no interest in partnering with Nubank, and the days continued to slip by. Finally, one bank agreed to collaborate, willing to support Nubank's innovative vision and provide the essential infrastructure for their operations.

With MasterCard and the partner bank on board, Nubank was close to fulfilling all the requirements needed for its launch. The entire team pushed hard to expedite the integration process, completing it at such a remarkable pace that Nubank became one of the fastest projects in MasterCard's history.[83] Meanwhile, the development team worked tirelessly on perfecting the app.

The Journey of the App

In addition to the card processor, Nubank needed other technology partners to provide various forms of connectivity. However, every collaboration attempt failed; potential partners

---

[83] SE Daily. Software Engineering Daily. Jul 2018. Podcast. "Build a Bank: Nubank with Edward Wible".
https://softwareengineeringdaily.com/2018/07/10/build-a-bank-nubank-with-edward-wible/

showed complete disinterest in working with the fledgling fintech.

Despite repeated rejections, the team remained undeterred. These setbacks only confirmed that the road ahead would be filled with challenges, continuously testing their resilience and determination.

Amid the relentless pressure, the development team pushed forward with the card application. Then, unexpectedly, they received a concerning yet cordial call from the Banking Commission: a regulatory change was on the horizon, potentially requiring them to obtain a banking license. To avoid this obstacle, Nubank needed to start operations as quickly as possible—before April 2014.

Applying for a banking license would have been a monumental undertaking, requiring at least three years—a timeframe that would have spelled the abrupt end of the project.

If you're not operating by April, you'll need to apply for a banking license to operate,

they warned with chilling frankness.

In other words, you'll be dead.

This ultimatum sparked a sense of terror and urgency.

In the carefully planned development timeline, everything was set to converge with the card launch in June 2014. However, the impending regulatory change forced them to accelerate their schedule, cutting out 60 critical days. David and the entire team shifted into "survival mode," revising strategies and executing precise actions to meet the new deadline. Yet, developing an app is never straightforward; programmers simply cannot work around the clock without rest.

As Edward Wibble recalled:

> *We pushed our engineers into full crisis mode, even offering them company stock bonuses if we met our deadline. And we did it!*

One of the key requirements for submitting the necessary documentation to the authorities was an official approval letter from MasterCard confirming they would be Nubank's processor. However, they had yet to receive this document. While MasterCard had agreed to provide it, the office responsible for issuing it was located in the Netherlands. After speaking with them, it became clear that the timeline for preparing the document and sending it to Brazil via courier would not work; it would arrive too late. Although MasterCard expedited the process of signing the document, the international courier service simply would not be fast enough.

To ensure they could deliver the approval letter to the authorities on time, the team decided the safest option was to personally fly to the Netherlands, retrieve the document by hand, and bring it back to Brazil.

The Launch Test

The initial launch of Nubank was filled with tension and anticipation. After a monumental effort by the development engineers to meet the deadline, they had barely slept, and problems continued to pile up, escalating stress and anxiety. Not only did they have to meet the tight deadline, but they also had to ensure they were building something of the highest quality, a product that could withstand scrutiny and deliver a flawless experience. Despite the mounting pressure, the clock kept ticking, and the day for the final tests arrived.

The first batch consisted of 12 cards, one for each employee, all of which were activated in the system and given credit lines so they could be used. With the app and cards ready, the connections with payment processors verified, and everything thoroughly reviewed—much like the meticulous pre-flight checks of a pilot—the only task left was to test everything in real life. The entire team, including the three founders, headed to the corner store with a mix of excitement and nerves, ready to test the cards. The plan was simple: each person would buy a coffee or a pastry.

However, in a cruel twist of fate, and true to Murphy's Law, the application failed. The first card was swiped, and the terminal returned the dreaded message: "Not Approved." Hoping it was just a fluke with the first card, they tried a second—and the same thing happened. Then a third, and another. Nothing happened. Someone likely broke the silence, stating what everyone was thinking: *Something is wrong; this isn't working.*

Everyone was disappointed, everyone was sad. We went home, David recalled of that moment. Time was running out, and they desperately needed the application to work. Without it, they would miss the window to launch before the regulatory change, and everything they had worked for would be lost. The sense of deep disappointment and anguish was palpable, but they knew they had to clear their heads and try again.

Despite the disheartening results of the previous day, resilience prevailed. The team returned to their computers, determined to uncover what had gone wrong. They meticulously combed through every detail until they identified the issues causing the transactions to be declined. Eventually, as is often the case, the problem was solved. With fingers crossed—perhaps even holding onto good luck charms—they headed back to the same store to test the cards once more. This time, someone recorded the moment. Everyone was wearing white T-shirts with the NU logo on the back, emblazoned with the slogan *Eu sobrevivi a implantação* (I survived the deployment). The engineers were so confident that this time it would work that Edward Wible chose bottles of some kind of sparkling wine as his purchase, ready to celebrate.

Cristina was the first to try her card. She inserted it into the terminal, typed her PIN, and... "Nao Autorizada" (Not Approved). In shock, Cristina repeated aloud, "Not authorized." Several engineers felt their hearts sink. Without a word, David stepped up next. He handed his card to the cashier, who inserted it into the terminal—nothing, declined again. Now it was Edward's turn, the last hope. It had to work. He pulled out his card, perhaps wondering if he should give it a rub for luck, and handed it to the cashier. She inserted the card and passed him the terminal. Edward entered his PIN, and...

"Autorizada" appeared on the screen. The transaction went through successfully, and the team exploded in cheers of excitement and… relief.[84]

That small victory brought immense relief and confirmed that they were on the right track. The engineers regained their confidence—they had built an application from scratch and made it work. They had met the deadline. And, as fate would have it, the third time truly was the charm.

Thus, on Tuesday, April 1, 2014, the first real transaction with a Nubank card was successfully completed, though the card would not be commercially available to the public until September of that year.

Traction

With the application up and running, the next step was to execute the marketing plan: launching a public relations campaign to introduce the purple card to consumers. David vividly recalls that day:

> *The day we announced the card and opened the website to the public, we made an internal bet on how many customers would sign up. Some guessed 1,500, others 1,000. One person*

---

[84] De Nuccio, Dony. InvestNews BR. Entrevista. May 2023. "Nubank mira em alta renda e Inteligência Artificial, diz Cris Junqueira". https://www.youtube.com/watch?v=b2q9BXhXJcQ&t=426s

even said 10,000. The average guess was about 1,000 customers.

The plan included promotion in high-circulation magazines. After considerable effort, they managed to secure a mention in a major magazine. The result? Only 200 customers.

We were completely disappointed and sad. There were many problems; we felt like everything was going wrong. Three months passed, and we only managed to get another 150 customers.

The year 2014 passed.

And then, one day, unexpectedly, a very niche publication talked about us.

It wasn't a major magazine or newspaper, not a business or financial publication. It was a publication aimed at the design and engineering community, but they decided to write about the purple card.

And suddenly, the next day we got 3,000 customers. he day after that, another 6,000. Then, 10,000 more.

Growth quickly spiraled out of control, catching the team completely off guard. The credit risk model wasn't yet fully developed, and they lacked sufficient data about their customers, so they could only approve around 15 to 20% of applicants. This meant that over 80% were receiving a rejection.

Then they had an idea: instead of saying *no*, they would say, *not yet*. The message became, *At this moment, we can't approve you, but in the next six months, we hope to say yes*. From that, another concept emerged: why not create a waiting list?[85]

They also decided that if someone was invited by an existing customer, they would receive priority on the waiting list. They viewed this as a recommendation, a positive indicator for their credit risk model.

This strategy allowed them to manage the explosive demand while simultaneously building a sense of exclusivity and anticipation among potential customers. The waiting list not only kept people engaged but also helped Nubank gather valuable data to further refine their credit risk assessments. What had initially seemed like an overwhelming challenge was transformed into a strategic advantage, laying the groundwork for Nubank's rapid growth and success.

The Waiting List Strategy

This strategy proved to be an excellent solution, as it eased the pressure to approve cards. However, it had an entirely

---

[85] Almeida, Marília. Exame. Minhas Financas. Sep 2015. "Conheça o Nubank, o cartão mais cobiçado do momento".
https://exame.com/invest/minhas-financas/conheca-o-nubank-cartao-mais-cobicado-do-momento/

unexpected side effect. The waiting list created a sense of virality and scarcity, triggering a desire to possess something perceived as exclusive—what only a few can have. This transformed the Nubank card into a coveted item. The scarcer it became, the more people wanted it. The demand didn't stop there; "recommendations" began to be sold on Mercado Libre.

This phenomenon of exclusivity and heightened desire worked in Nubank's favor, generating even greater interest and a rapidly growing waiting list. The deliberate strategy of controlling and moderating card issuance not only allowed Nubank to better manage risk and operational capacity but also helped create an image of prestige and exclusivity around their product. The combination of scarcity and high demand provided a significant boost to the brand, solidifying its position in the market and attracting more customers eager to get their hands on the coveted card.

By the end of 2018, Nubank had 14 million people on the waiting list, while customers who already had their card spent an average of $192 USD per month.[86]

David recalled:

> *At that moment, I began to realize—on that very day when everything exploded and so many people wanted the card—WOW, okay. There is something here. We had created the most democratic credit card, saying yes to those whom other banks had rejected.*

---

[86] Cfr. Chu, Michael, et al. Harvard Business School. Caso 9-321-068. Rev. Ago 2023. "Nubank: Democratizing Financial Services"

The good news was that things were moving, and moving well. The adjusted original goal was to reach one million customers in five years, but to their surprise, they achieved it in just two. They then set a new goal: ten million customers in five years. Once again, they reached it in just two.

But the challenges were far from over; they were still lurking, waiting for their moment.

Liquidity Crisis

The growth was so rapid that it far exceeded all initial forecasts, which quickly became a significant problem. As more credit was granted, the internal capital requirements skyrocketed, and the necessary liquidity to sustain this expansion had not been anticipated. There simply wasn't enough cash flow to finance the growth. The only option was to seek additional investors—this time focusing on local ones, thinking that now, with clear evidence the business was working, investors would be eager to get involved. But there was no interest; every potential investor they approached gave a definitive "no," stating it was "too risky." In a way, they were right: by traditional standards, Nubank did not fit conventional risk models.

Once again, David packed his bags and returned to the United States in search of liquidity. But as was often the case, it was not easy. After visiting many investors, at the last moment, Goldman Sachs stepped in and offered them a special line of credit, tailored to meet their urgent needs. This infusion of capital allowed Nubank to acquire another 100,000 customers, and soon after, they reached an additional 200,000. The line of credit proved to be a game changer for Nubank, and later on, Citi Bank joined in as well. To this day, this strategy remains a crucial part of Nubank's financial approach.

In the normal course of business, customers used their cards daily, making various purchases. According to industry standards, Nubank was required to pay merchants every 30 days for all the purchases made by its customers during that period. Naturally, as the number of customers grew, so did the volume of purchases, and consequently, the amount Nubank needed to pay merchants increased steadily.

One Friday morning, while David was in Washington D.C., enjoying breakfast and reading the newspaper, he came across a headline that nearly made him drop his coffee. The Brazilian Senate was considering a regulation change that would reduce the payment period for merchants from 30 days to just 2 days.

The note read:

> *Retailers and service providers will have a maximum of two business days to receive the amounts of sales made via credit card. This is established by Senate Bill (PLS) 344/2018, which will be reviewed in a final decision by the Economic Affairs Committee (CAE).*

Currently, merchants had to wait 30 days to receive the funds from credit card sales via acquirers. David was stunned as he realized the implications for Nubank. They would suddenly need around 1 billion Brazilian reais—approximately $300 million USD—on top of their existing liquidity needs, and of course, they didn't have that kind of capital readily available.

This news posed a serious threat to Nubank's financial stability. The proposed regulation had the potential to destabilize their operations entirely, putting the company's survival at risk. Faced with this urgent crisis, David and his team had no choice but to act swiftly.

They quickly reached out to their investors and financial partners, explaining the situation and seeking potential solutions. Simultaneously, they began working on mitigation strategies to ensure that if the regulation passed, they could still meet the new requirements without jeopardizing the company's financial health.

Raising that amount of money in just a week was nearly impossible. At that time, Nubank already had over 6 million customers. David rushed to the office to brainstorm with the entire team about alternative solutions. Given the clear impossibility of securing such a vast sum, they needed to think outside the box and come up with something completely different. That's when the idea of a social pressure strategy was born.

Most of Nubank's employees were millennials, deeply familiar with social media. They decided to first go to the press, highlighting the devastating effect this regulation would have on Nubank—potentially forcing them out of business. They argued that the big banks were behind the push for this change in an effort to drive Nubank out of the financial sector, which was true. They portrayed Nubank as the hero in this story, a company offering low fees and interest rates, treating customers fairly, and enjoying the support of millions of satisfied users.

In addition, they launched a Twitter campaign that generated thousands of tweets directed at the Central Bank of Brazil, urging them not to implement the change. The response was overwhelming. Nubank users, as well as many others, rallied in defense of the fintech, sharing their positive experiences and voicing support against what they saw as an unfair attack by traditional banks.

This wave of social and media pressure created a substantial impact. The Central Bank of Brazil and the legislators could not ignore the groundswell of public support for Nubank and the widespread concern over the consequences of the proposed regulation.

David recalls a pivotal meeting around noon with the president of the Central Bank.

My co-founders and I sat down across from him, and as soon as we took our seats, the president spoke:

— 'Calm down, calm down, don't worry, this isn't going to happen.

—Everything is fine.

—*Let's talk now about how you can continue competing because we like competition. You're having a good impact on the country.'*

The president of the Central Bank continued saying:

—*'You're saving people billions of dollars in fees, granting credit and products to people who never had access before. We like what you're doing and want to encourage it. Over the past 10 years, Brazil has been working to foster competition across the country, and much of the regulation reflects that commitment.*

The pressure had been so intense that the Central Bank ultimately decided not to implement the change. It was a huge scare, but they managed to avert disaster.

Years later, the Central Bank did implement the reform, reducing the payment time to merchants to two days, but by then, Nubank was well prepared.

This experience also confirmed that the culture David had worked to instill at Nubank was thriving. As David often said, *We want fans, not customers.*

The Brazilian Banking License

Nubank was expanding rapidly, and its status as a Payment Institution was becoming restrictive. To continue growing, they needed something more—so they decided to apply for a banking license.

Any financial institution that accepts deposits from the general public and thus assumes direct responsibility to its customers requires specific authorization from the financial regulatory authority. The authorization to operate as a bank is one of the most comprehensive and significantly broadens the range of products that can be offered. For instance, if Nubank wanted to provide savings accounts, a banking license was essential.

Obtaining a banking license is no simple feat; it represents a significant barrier to entry. To qualify, a company must meet stringent capitalization requirements, implement robust security systems, and adhere to rigorous controls, especially those related to preventing money laundering and the financing of terrorism. In Brazil, the challenge was even greater, with strict regulations designed to protect the domestic financial sector, including a prohibition against foreign ownership or investment in Brazilian banks.

This obstacle appeared nearly impossible to overcome. However, Nubank represented a fresh and innovative force in the industry. David and his team understood that to break through this barrier, they would need strong local support. They began forging strategic alliances and cultivating relationships with influential figures in the Brazilian financial landscape.

Simultaneously, Nubank worked on multiple fronts to satisfy all the requirements for obtaining the banking license. At the same time, they launched a campaign to emphasize the advantages of allowing a forward-thinking company like Nubank to fully operate in the Brazilian market.

With the help of lawyers and numerous visits to the Central Bank, Nubank sought to obtain a Presidential Decree, signed directly by the President of Brazil, granting them an exception to the prohibition on foreign investment. Given that Citi, Santander, and HSBC were already operating in the country, there were legal precedents to support their efforts in securing such an exemption.

On January 19, 2018, after four long years, Nubank finally received the much-anticipated banking license.[87] The most time-consuming aspect of the process was waiting for the president's signature on the decree, which sat on his desk for nearly eight months before it was finally signed.

According to the statement published in the Official Gazette, the President of Brazil, Michel Temer, approved Decree 9,544, which explicitly states:

> *(...) it is in the interest of the Brazilian government to have up to 100% foreign ownership in the share capital of the financial*

---

[87] Brazil, presidential decree of banking license to Nubank. Jan 2018. http://www.planalto.gov.br/ccivil_03/_ato2015-2018/2018/dsn/Dsn14509.htm

institution to be formed by NU Holdings Ltd., located in the Cayman Islands.[88]

The banking license marked a major milestone for Nubank. Not only did it allow them to expand their product offerings, but it also solidified their commitment to the country, reassuring any Brazilians who might have questioned their long-term intentions. It was their official entry into Brazil's financial landscape, symbolizing their full integration into the country's economic fabric.

However, this license, granted by the Central Bank of Brazil, also heightened the existing tension within the Brazilian banking system, as traditional banks now faced direct and formidable competition from fintechs like Nubank.

Mexico

David commented:

I went to Mexico in 2015, came back super excited, saying we had to go to Mexico. What a great market. But the Board of Directors (...) told me: —Stop!

—"You're not ready. You don't have a financing product. You don't have a license.

---

[88] Baria, Steven. S&P Global. Fintech. Juan 2018. "Nubank's Brazil operation approved by President Temer".
https://www.spglobal.com/marketintelligence/en/news-insights/trending/frgo6ztqrh196ojfnysnrq2

You're not profitable. It's too early. You're going to get sidetracked."

And that was the right advice. It was too early for us. We stopped the project completely and focused on building the deposit product.

Three years later, by 2018, our critical product was profitable. We had a banking license. We already had deposits.

We were growing very fast. By then, we felt ready to take on a second market. At that point, we decided we could start building our operations in Mexico.[89]

In May 2019, Nubank embarked on the second phase of its journey: international expansion. The company set its sights on Mexico, the second-largest country in Latin America with a population of 126 million.

Mexican regulations required Nubank to make several modifications to its business model, starting with its branding. Since the word "bank" could only be used by institutions with a banking license, Nubank entered the market under the name NU Mexico.

---

[89] Cfr. Morris, Nigel. Entrevista con David. Fintech Nexus. Jun 2022. Nubank (Full Session)"
https://www.youtube.com/watch?v=yXLWiePLt6U

During an interview in Mexico, David discussed the strategic decision to enter this market, offering a candid assessment of its potential and challenges:

We have studied the Mexican financial system for several years and listened to many consumers talk about the frustrations and difficulties they encounter with the existing services.

These services have neglected to prioritize the consumer in their strategy and product offerings.

Moreover, over 36 million Mexicans currently lack access to the banking system, and we want to play a role in changing that.[90]

Their first product in Mexico was the iconic purple credit card. Launching operations in 2019 under the corporate name NU BN Servicios México, S.A. de C.V., they announced an investment of $135 million to establish their presence and grow their business in the country.[91]

Later, in order to offer their savings product, NU sought approval from the authorities to acquire a SOFIPO (Sociedad

---

[90] Nubank, Redacción. NU México. "NU llega a México con servicios financieros digitales"
https://blog.nu.com.mx/prensa-nubank-llega-a-mexico/#
[91] Gutiérrez, Fernando. El Economista. Sector Financiero. Sep 2021. "El unicornio crece, NU México compra sofipo Akala".
https://www.eleconomista.com.mx/sectorfinanciero/El-unicornio-crece-NU-Mexico-compra-sofipo-Akala-20210921-0033.html

Financiera Popular).[92] In September 2021, they purchased Sofipo Akala, a defunct entity owned by Grupo Progreso, the parent company of Bankaool, for $3 million.[93] By mid-2020, Akala had already ceased operations and had no remaining customers, making it an ideal acquisition for NU. In February 2022, they received authorization to rename the entity NU México Financiera.

Shortly thereafter, due to NU's remarkable growth, regulatory authorities began requesting extensive information through nearly 20 formal inquiries. In just over a year of operation, NU had become the leader in the SOFIPO sector, amassing more than 5.1 million customers and $26 billion Mexican pesos in assets—representing almost 36% of the entire popular financial sector.

Growth

---

[92] SOFIPO is a Popular Financial Society, regulated and supervised by the regulatory authority in Mexico, the National Banking and Securities Commission (CNBV). Its main purpose is to offer financial services to segments of the population that are not fully served by traditional banks. Among its most common functions and services are: savings collection, credit granting, offering investment services, and providing payment and money transfer services.

[93] Gutiérrez, Fernando. DiaFintech. Enero 2024. "¿Qué información le ha pedido la CNBV a NU México ya como sofipo?"
https://diafintech.com.mx/que-informacion-le-ha-pedido-la-cnbv-a-nu-mexico-ya-como-sofipo/#:~:text=Recordemos%20que%2C%20en%20septiembre%20del,para%20integrarse%20al%20mundo%20regulado.

NU signed up 500,000 customers within the first two weeks of launching its purple credit card in Mexico.[94] Within a year, NU had become the largest issuer of credit cards in the country, boasting a staggering year-over-year growth rate of 1,243%.

By the end of 2023, NU México had grown to 5.2 million customers, with deposits exceeding $1 billion, while maintaining a delinquency rate of 10.26%, down from 12.40% in the last quarter of 2022.

By 2024, NU México had issued over 7 million cards, with a large percentage of its customers receiving their first-ever credit card through Nubank. Despite low credit card usage in Mexico, where only 10% of adults aged 18 to 70 had a bank-issued credit card and 20% had a department store credit card, Nubank made significant strides. In comparison, credit card penetration in Brazil stood at 40%.

According to the Bank of Mexico, the credit card delinquency rate had risen to 9.5% by June 2023.[95]

Investment and Expansion

---

[94] InvestNews BR. May 2023. "Nubank mira em alta renda e Inteligência Artificial, diz Cris Junqueira".
https://www.youtube.com/watch?v=b2q9BXkXkcQ
[95] According to information from the Bank of Mexico, as of the end of September 2023, the balance of overdue consumer loans (which include credit cards, debit cards, payroll loans, among other instruments) reached a total of 40.108 billion pesos, 42 percent higher than what was reported in September of the previous year.

Nubank continued to make significant investments in its Mexican operations. In December 2022, the company announced a $330 million investment to expand its product portfolio and extend its market reach. This was followed by an additional $100 million investment in 2024,[96] reinforcing Mexico as a priority market for the company. These investments have positioned NU México as one of the best-capitalized financial institutions in the country.

Additionally, NU recognized that Mexico was not only a promising market but also home to a high concentration of talented engineers. Reflecting on this, David remarked:

> *We have been impressed with the level of talent in Mexico, and we are eager to make a significant investment in the Mexican tech ecosystem.*

> *David explained:*

> *Mexico is different from the other two countries where we operate. The difference between a SOFIPO and a bank is substantial. There are many things a bank can do that a SOFIPO cannot. In Brazil, under the current regulations, there is virtually no distinction between the equivalent of a financial institution and a bank (…) in Mexico, however, we clearly see the need for this distinction, which is why*

---

[96] Cota, Isabel. ELPAIS. Abr 2024. "Nubank inyecta 100 millones de dólares a su operación en México" https://elpais.com/mexico/economia/2024-04-16/nubank-inyectara-100-millones-de-dolares-a-su-operacion-en-mexico.html

we have decided to take the next step and apply for a banking license.[97]

Nubank's success in Mexico can also be attributed to its customer-focused approach and its innovative financial products, which outperformed those offered by traditional banks. Although Mexican banks had already begun responding to the digital revolution by adopting and mimicking some of NU's concepts, Nubank viewed Mexico as an ideal market for growth in the region. This was not only because Mexico is the second-largest country in Latin America but also because it lagged behind in key metrics such as banking penetration, reliance on cash, and credit card usage. They also recognized that, in Mexico, credit cards are primarily used as credit instruments, unlike in Brazil.

Nubank's founder mentioned that they had engaged with members of the Mexican Banking Association (ABM), who expressed optimism about NU's transition to becoming a bank. However, there was some pressure from traditional banks due to NU's status as a SOFIPO, which, being less regulated than a bank, placed them at a competitive disadvantage.

When we apply for a banking license, we are clearly stating: we want to play by the same rules, on the same field. We have no interest in operating a banking business without actually being a bank. We see it as a positive step to be

---

[97] Juárez, Edgar. El Economista. Sector Financiero. Mar 2024. "NU: "no vemos razón para no poder ser uno de los bancos más importantes de México" https://www.eleconomista.com.mx/sectorfinanciero/NU-no-vemos-razon-para-no-poder-ser-uno-de-los-bancos-mas-importantes-de-Mexico-20240304-0091.html

regulated just like the other members of the system, and we are confident that, even within this regulatory framework, we can continue to compete effectively.

In Mexico, NU has concentrated its efforts on promoting financial inclusion by offering products like the digital savings account "Cuenta NU," which includes a feature called "Cajitas" (little boxes). This functionality allows customers to create up to 10 separate sections to better organize their savings, with each section earning the same daily interest. NU initially attracted customers by offering an unprecedented 15% annual interest rate on savings, a rate that no other institution in Mexico had provided. However, in response to market conditions, NU adjusted the rate to 14.5% in June and then to 14.25% in July 2024.

What truly set NU apart was the simplicity and transparency it brought to saving. Customers could deposit or withdraw money at any time without restrictions, complex procedures, or lengthy contracts. Additionally, the "Cajitas" feature offered a tax exemption for up to $189,222 pesos or $10,000 per year (5 UMAs),[98] with a tax rate of 0.5% applied to any excess.

---

[98] UMA: Unidad de Medida y Actualización, an Unit of Measurement and Update on inflation, is an economic reference in Mexico used to calculate fines, credits, taxes, and other payments established in federal and local laws. It was created to decouple these payments from the minimum wage, thereby avoiding inflationary impacts on workers' incomes. In 2024, the annual UMA was valued at $37,844.40 pesos. Approximately two thousand dollars.

David believes that offering 15% yield rates is feasible, citing the substantial margins made possible by their fully digital operation.

According to him,

It is just a matter of doing the math.

If you capture funds at zero and lend at 70 or 80%, you're looking at enormous margins. Even at 15%, there is still a substantial margin. In our case, with a 100% digital operation, those margins remain very favorable. David explained.[99]

NU Mexico's impact goes far beyond its product offerings. It has played a vital role in advancing financial education, with 45% of its customers obtaining their first credit card through Nubank. NU Mexico has also achieved remarkable customer satisfaction, ranking first in KPMG's Customer Experience Study.

Nubank's success in Mexico reflects its commitment to simplicity and transparency. Within the first two weeks of its launch, it signed up 500,000 customers and quickly became one of the largest credit card issuers in the country, boasting a growth rate of 1,243% by the end of 2021. By 2024, NU Mexico had issued over 7 million cards.

---

[99] Cfr. Juárez, Edgar. El Economista. Sector Financiero. Mar 2024.

The competition in Mexico's financial sector is fierce. By the end of 2023, the country had 36 SOFIPOs and 713 fintechs in operation.[100]

In October 2023, NU applied for a banking license with the CNBV, aiming to establish itself as a key player in the Mexican financial landscape by responding to its customers' needs and providing solutions that simplify the financial lives of millions.

Colombia

Nubank's third expansion took place in Colombia on February 24, 2021. With over 51 million inhabitants, Colombia presented unique challenges for the company.

David reflected on this move, saying:

> Colombia has been the most difficult country to enter; of the three—Brazil, Mexico, and Colombia—it is the most complicated, not only from a macroeconomic standpoint but also from a regulatory perspective. It has the most friction in terms of entry, regulation, and competition. It's a complex ocean to navigate, but we are having productive conversations with regulators to establish a regulatory

---

[100] Finnovista. Radar México. Feb 2024.
https://www.finnovista.com/radar/actualizacion-octava-edicion-finnovista-fintech-radar-mexico/

agenda that fosters and grows the fintech ecosystem.[101]

As in Mexico, Nubank's first product launch in Colombia was its signature purple credit card. The launch was done in true NU style, with 50,000 of these cards delivered in a unique welcome kit. Instead of a standard envelope, customers received their cards in a specially designed purple box created by the artist *Ledania*.[102] Each box contained a numbered and signed collectible illustration by the artist, representing the water goddess Sie from Muisca mythology.[103] The illustration, crafted in plastic acrylic, included a 1,000 Colombian pesos coin alongside a message that read: *The 1,000 Colombian pesos coin represents the cash we use every day. In the future, it will be a collector's item.* This reference hinted at the eventual disappearance of cash from daily transactions. The box's sides, featuring Ledania's graffiti art, contrasted with the purple lids.

---

[101] Benito, Luis. Infobae. Colombia. Ene 2024. "Nubank, el banco del hombre más rico de Colombia, sacude el mercado: lanzó su cuenta de ahorros en el país".
https://www.infobae.com/colombia/2024/01/17/nubank-el-banco-del-hombre-mas-rico-de-colombia-sacude-el-mercado-lanzo-su-cuenta-de-ahorros-en-el-pais/

[102] Diana Ordóñez, better known as Ledania, is a Colombian plastic artist, born in Bogotá. She dedicated to painting graffiti and murals around the world.

[103] Muisca mythology belongs to the culture of the Muiscas, an indigenous people who inhabited the central region of Colombia, mainly in the highlands of Cundiboyacense. Their mythology is rich in stories that explain the creation of the world, natural phenomena, and the lives of the gods and heroes of their culture.

The 50,000 customers[104] who received this special kit were randomly selected from the first 300,000 applicants for the card.

Santiago Eastman, NU designer and creator of the project, explained:

> *This welcome kit is the gateway to a new world—the NU world—where we do things differently and work alongside Colombians to shape the future of financial services. We didn't want to just create an object; we wanted to craft an experience that surprises and intrigues people, but most importantly, reflects the transition from the past to the future of money in our country.*

By May 2024, Nubank Colombia had grown rapidly, reaching 900,000 customers.

Product Expansion

The second product was their Savings Account, which already had a waiting list of over 500,000 people.[105] In January 2024, the Financial Superintendence of Colombia authorized

---

[104] Semana. Bancos. Jul 2021. "NU Colombia repartirá 50.000 tarjetas cargadas de arte"
https://www.semana.com/economia/empresas/articulo/nu-colombia-repartira-50000-tarjetas-cargadas-de-arte-le-contamos-los-detalles-de-la-iniciativa/202150/

[105] NU, NU Colombia. May 2024. "NU Holdings Ltd. reporta los resultados financieros del primer trimestre del 2024"
https://blog.nu.com.co/resultados-nu-holdings-2024-1/

the establishment of NU Colombia Compañía de Financiamiento, a new entity created to support the Savings Account.[106] The account will offer an annual effective yield of 13%,[107] the highest in the Colombian market, along with free transfers to any financial institution.

According to a NU analysis, *more than 50% of Colombians encounter barriers to saving with existing products, either due to low perceived returns or because their money fails to grow as a result of management fees and other associated costs.*[108]

David mentioned that Colombia posed the most complex regulatory challenge among the three countries in which NU operates.

NU has established an engineering, product, and data science center in Colombia to develop the next generation of financial services in the country.

From the outset, Nubank has invested heavily in the Colombian market. In December 2022, the company

---

[106] Sánchez, Camilo. El País. América Colombia. Jun 2024. "El digital Nubank irrumpe como principal banco de América Latina" https://elpais.com/america-colombia/2024-06-03/el-digital-nubank-irrumpe-como-principal-banco-de-america-latina.html

[107] The term "E.A." It is commonly used in finance in Colombia to express annual interest rates that take into account the capitalization of interest.

[108] Benito, Luis. Infobae. Colombia. Ene 2024. "Nubank, el banco del hombre más rico de Colombia, sacude el mercado: lanzó su cuenta de ahorros en el país".
https://www.infobae.com/colombia/2024/01/17/nubank-el-banco-del-hombre-mas-rico-de-colombia-sacude-el-mercado-lanzo-su-cuenta-de-ahorros-en-el-pais/

announced a capitalization of $330 million to expand its product portfolio and increase penetration across different market segments. This investment has positioned Nubank as one of the best-capitalized financial institutions in Colombia.

Challenges and Future

Nubank's biggest challenges include targeting the high-income population. They understand this will not happen overnight, but they are developing a compelling value proposition to genuinely attract and engage this audience. Another challenge is continuing to grow in Mexico and Colombia, aiming to introduce the same products they offer in Brazil, with necessary adjustments for each market. Fortunately, they already have a solid product portfolio to build upon.

These are significant undertakings because, while growth can be achieved with a credit card, in the beginning, only a certain segment of customers can be approved. Many cannot receive credit either because they are not well-known, have poor credit histories, or are burdened by debt.

When a customer applies for a debit card, they are automatically given the option to open a savings account, providing everyone with the opportunity to start saving. For NU, this product has transformed their ability to acquire customers. Mexico and Colombia represent major growth opportunities.[109]

Following tradition, NU has also encountered challenges in Colombia with its operations.

Some of the difficulties in this market include closed interbank transfer systems,[110] a lack of financial literacy among citizens, and the constraints imposed by the Usury Rate.[111] Expanding beyond financial services presents an intriguing opportunity, although it may not be the most obvious one. David notes that he has seen numerous examples worldwide of commercial companies moving into financial services or social media businesses entering the sector. Alibaba is a prime example, and Tencent[112] is another, with its ecosystem that includes WeChat, Riot Games, Epic Games, WeChat Pay, QQ Wallet, and more. However, this movement from financial

---

[109] InvestNews BR. Entrevista Cristina Junqueira. May 2023. "Nubank mira em alta renda e Inteligência Artificial, diz Cris Junqueira".
https://www.youtube.com/watch?v=b2q9BXkXkcQ

[110] In Colombia, "closed circuits" in interbank transfers refer to specific networks of banks that have agreements among themselves to facilitate the direct transfer of funds between their customers without the need to go through a centralized clearinghouse. This system only works among the banks that are part of the circuit and is not public, unlike in Mexico.

[111] The Usury Rate in Colombia is a regulatory tool. It is the maximum limit allowed by law for the interest that financial institutions can charge for loans and credits. This rate is calculated quarterly and is set by the Financial Superintendence of Colombia. The problem with this rate is that it is not a market rate; it is fixed and does not always facilitate access to credit, reduce the cost of financing, or promote financial inclusion.

[112] Tencent Holdings Ltd. is a Chinese multinational technology conglomerate and holding company based in Shenzhen. It is one of the world's largest multimedia companies in terms of revenue. https://www.tencent.com/en-us/about.html

services into commerce has not been observed to the same degree.

Several factors could encourage this shift. The first is the strong brand and trust that many financial institutions have established. Managing people's money and bank accounts is no small responsibility, and there is a deep emotional connection between these institutions and their customers.

The Co-founders

Cristina Junqueira

Cristina Helena Zingaretti Junqueira is one of the brilliant minds behind Nubank, serving as the Chief Growth Officer. In this role, she is responsible for orchestrating operations and crafting growth strategies in Mexico and Colombia, helping to bring NU's financial innovations to new markets. Additionally, she oversees marketing and communications, consolidating Nubank's brand and presence. Her vision and leadership are pivotal to the company's ongoing success and expansion across Latin America.

Born in 1982 in São Paulo, Brazil, Cristina has built a family with her husband, Rubens Pereira, and their three daughters. What has captured the attention of the international press is Cristina's remarkable ability to balance her personal and professional life with exceptional skill, especially in such a demanding role.

Cristina has noted that her daughters were born during pivotal—and often stressful—moments in Nubank's early days. During the company's first funding round in 2014, Cristina signed the documents from the hospital while in active labor! In 2021, as Nubank went public, an iconic photograph shows Cristina visibly pregnant alongside her co-founders at the New York Stock Exchange. Her daughter was born just days after this historic event.

Cristina's ability to seamlessly combine motherhood and business leadership has made her an inspiring figure across Latin America. Her story not only underscores her financial success but also her resilience and dedication, redefining what it means to be a female entrepreneur in the 21st century.

With a 3% stake in Nubank,[113] Cristina has amassed an estimated fortune of $1.5 billion,[114] making her the first woman in the region to become a billionaire through her own achievements—a true self-made billionaire.

Cristina began her academic journey at the prestigious Polytechnic School of the University of São Paulo (USP), where she earned a degree in engineering and completed a master's in economics and financial modeling in 2006. At 24, she started her career at the consulting firm Booz Allen, followed by a role at the Boston Consulting Group, where she gained valuable experience in strategic consulting.

In 2007, driven by a desire to expand her knowledge and skills, Cristina pursued an MBA at the Kellogg School of Management at Northwestern University.

Upon her return to Brazil in 2008, Cristina took on an executive role at Unibanco, the largest private banking group in the country at the time. During her tenure, she witnessed and participated in the historic merger with Itaú, which led to the creation of Itaú Unibanco, one of Brazil's financial giants.

---

[113] Forbes Profile. Cristina Junqueira. May 2024. https://www.forbes.com/profile/Cristina-junqueira/?sh=4f5918c78d9d
[114] Cfr. BBC News Mundo. Dic.2021. "Quién es Cristina Junqueira, la primera multimillonaria de América Latina que fundó una empresa desde cero". https://www.bbc.com/mundo/noticias-59598369

Cristina later transitioned to LuizaCred,[115] and subsequently to Itaú Banco, where she served as Manager at Itaucard. Over five years, she immersed herself in the traditional world of Brazilian banking, gaining deep insights into the financial sector and credit cards—knowledge she would later draw upon in co-founding Nubank.

Despite her success in the banking industry, Cristina began to feel unfulfilled. After launching a new campaign for a product that was essentially the same as its predecessors, she had a revelation: *I thought it was an unsustainable business.* The product had high fees and interest rates and relied on aggressive telemarketing to sell—a model she found deeply flawed.

Determined to make a meaningful change, Cristina took the opportunity to design a pilot project that significantly improved the product's appeal. Instead of the traditional "push" approach of aggressive sales, her model was based on "pull," focusing on offering a better product that would naturally attract more willing customers.

With her project ready for launch, Cristina presented it to her Senior Vice President. Within half an hour, he flatly rejected it.[116] For Cristina, this was the final straw.

In March 2013, she made a momentous decision: despite receiving a substantial bonus for her work,[117] she resigned from

---

[115] LuizaCred was a company that sought to facilitate access to credit for consumers, allowing more people to purchase products in the stores of Magazine Luiza, a chain of appliance and electronics stores in Brazil, through accessible and personalized financing options. It was a joint venture between the Magazine Luiza group and Unibanco (currently part of Itaú Unibanco).
[116] Chu, Michael, et al. Harvard Business School. Caso "Nubank: Democratizing Financial services" 2020. Rev. Aug 2023.
[117] Leaders. Person Cristina Junqueira. Jun 2023.

her position at Itaú Bank. Reflecting on her career, Cristina realized she had spent her efforts enriching those who were already wealthy, without achieving the consumer-focused changes she longed to make. *I was done*, she said. *I wanted to give myself space to think about what I would do in the next years of my life.*[118]

At this pivotal moment, fate intervened to change both Cristina and David's lives.

Roelof Botha,[119] a partner at Sequoia, had advised David that he needed a co-founder with deep banking experience in Brazil. With that advice in mind, David accepted a mutual acquaintance's suggestion to meet Cristina.

Cristina had all the right qualities: she was a consummate professional with an intimate knowledge of the Brazilian banking system and extensive experience managing credit cards. She also had a strong desire to become an entrepreneur. Having just left Itaú Bank, she was perfectly poised for a new challenge.

When they met, David shared his vision with her. As Cristina listened, she felt a powerful draw toward the idea of creating a bank. What David was proposing was not the typical *let's start something* or *why don't we see what's happening in the U.S. or Europe?* These were not the vague ideas friends toss around over drinks that ultimately lead nowhere.

David's proposal was entirely different. It was serious, well thought out, and directly addressed the real problems consumers had faced for decades—the very issues Cristina had

---

https://leaders.com/rankings/person/Cristina-junqueira/
[118] Cfr. International Finance Corporation. Latin Focus. Nov 2023.
[119] Cfr. International Finance Corporation. Latin Focus. Nov 2023.

CO-FOUNDERS

seen throughout her career. These problems had become so ingrained in daily life that people had stopped questioning them. *That's just how it is, that's how it's always worked* they would say. But when David laid out these issues, it was as if a veil had been lifted. *Of course,* Cristina thought, *these are the problems that need to be solved!* [120]

David's clarity and depth in his proposal resonated with Cristina. Her determination to transform the financial sector found a perfect match in David's vision. Together, they decided to embark on the ambitious journey of founding Nubank.

Cristina later reflected:[121]

— *Why did I accept?*
— *Because I was in the right place at the right time; it was one of those 'serendipity moments.'*

— *It was a great opportunity to prove many people wrong. I couldn't pass it up. I remember thinking, 'Well, if there was anyone in this country who could really pull this off, it was me.' I had other offers, and this one, from a financial point of view, was by far the least attractive—since I had to invest my own money—but it was too great an opportunity to ignore.* [122]

And so, they began their work.

---
[120] Op. Cit. Novak, Turner. The Peel.
[121] Fortune Magazine. Entrevista. Sep 2019. "Nubank Wants to Break Up Big Banks in Latin America".
https://www.youtube.com/watch?v=Dc4Vg5GBTzU
[122] Op. Cit. Novak, Turner. The Peel.

Cristina has broken numerous barriers throughout her career. As mentioned earlier, during Nubank's Series A round, she flew from Brazil to California to pitch to investors. One of them remarked, "*Oh, I've never seen a pregnant woman pitching.*" Cristina was seven months pregnant at the time. She recalls that round as incredibly intense, if not exhausting, but she had unwavering faith that things would turn out well. Still, it was not easy—most investors ended up saying no.

Despite the challenges, the team eventually raised $15 million in their Series A round, led by Sequoia, in August 2014. In a particularly memorable moment, David brought the investment documents to the hospital for Cristina to sign while she was in labor with Elli, her first daughter. It was a testament to her unrelenting commitment and determination.

Being pregnant during Nubank's growth did pose concerns for Cristina. At first, she tried to keep it under wraps, but it quickly became impossible to hide. Cristina knew that, as co-founder, she had responsibilities to both clients and shareholders, and she took them seriously.

She made history as the first visibly pregnant woman to appear on the cover of a Brazilian business magazine, just days before the birth of her second daughter.[123] In 2020, she was recognized as one of Brazil's most powerful women by Forbes and was the only Brazilian to appear on Fortune's "40 under 40" list that year.[124]

---

[123] Forbes Brasil. Mar 2020. "As mulheres mais poderosas do Brasil em 2020" https://forbes.com.br/listas/2020/03/as-mulheres-mais-poderosas-do-brasil-em-2020/
[124] FORTUNE, Sep 2020. "Fortune's 2020 40 Under 40 List – Finance". https://fortune.com/videos/watch/fortune's-2020-40-under-40-list---finance/b2d4be91-a188-4fe7-a58c-05663670b332

Nubank's growth has been remarkably rapid, especially when compared to other digital banks. It is now the largest digital bank in the world by customer base, excluding Chinese banks. Cristina attributes this success to a simple fact: *nobody likes banks*. In many parts of the world, some banks are truly despised. *If you Google 'do people hate banks in Brazil?' in Portuguese, you'll find pages and pages of complaints,* Cristina explains. This is the result of decades of abuses, excessive fees, poor products, and even worse customer service, combined with Brazil's notoriously high interest rates—the highest in the world.

An article published by Brazil's Intercept in 2019 encapsulated what Cristina was referring to: consumers were fed up with traditional banking services, and Nubank emerged as a fresh, customer-friendly alternative that broke away from the entrenched practices of the old banking sector. Cristina and her team's vision has been instrumental in positioning Nubank as a leader in the digital financial revolution in Latin America.

One particularly striking headline read:

BANKS PROFIT WHILE FAMILIES SUFFER PAYING THE BILLS.

December 24, 2019 — Financial suffering devastates families in Brazil, where banks reap the most obscene profits in the world, even as the country remains in economic crisis... [125]

Cristina had experienced this firsthand and recalls telling her partners,

---

[125] Op.Cit. Fortune Magazine. Entrevista. Sep 2019. "Nubank Wants to Break Up Big Banks in Latin America"

> *We have to be prepared to spend a lot of money on marketing because people hate banks.*[126]

So, when an alternative finally appeared, many customers did not hesitate to switch.

> *Many even asked Nubank to allow their friends and family to join. Our own clients referred more clients to us, completely organically,*

Cristina explained in an interview,

> *The great advantage was the size of the Brazilian market—210 million people, with 60 million unbanked. The opportunity was enormous, but also more accessible due to the struggles that potential customers were facing with traditional banks.*

By that time, Nubank had already saved its customers nearly 8 billion dollars in "junk fees" in just one year—money that allowed their clients to reduce their cost of living in meaningful ways.

In the same interview, Cristina was asked if she believed this model could work in North America. She responded,

---

[126] Intercep_Brasil. Pinheiro-Machado, Rosana. Dic 2019. "Bancos lucram enquanto famílias sofrem pagando boletos".
https://www.intercept.com.br/2019/12/24/sofrimento-financeiro-bancos-boletos/

It is true that those who suffer the most from banking are in Latin America. In Canada, the United States, or even Europe, banking is not as expensive. For NU, it is a matter of sequence and priority—we see more opportunity in Latin America because that is where the pain is greatest. But the fact remains that everything is moving digital. Worldwide, consumers want to handle everything on their smartphones and never step foot in a branch again, and that trend is not going away.[127]

Cristina emphasizes that Nubank is deeply committed to its values, especially challenging the status quo and maintaining a "beginner's mind." One of the company's biggest challenges remains human capital. Although Nubank's teams are diverse, with more than 40% of its workforce being women, they are constantly looking for more talent across all their offices.

Cristina Junqueira emphasizes that Nubank is obsessive about its values, particularly in challenging the status quo and fostering a *beginner's mind* mentality. One of their key challenges is attracting human capital. Although their teams are diverse, with over 40% women, they are constantly seeking more talent across all their offices.

---

[127] MasterCard News, Entrevista. Abr. 2024. "Nubank's incredible journey in financial inclusion with Cristina Junqueira and Linda Kirkpatrick". https://www.youtube.com/watch?v=CivjKeqQJpmc

Edward Wible

Adam Edward Wible was born in Austin, Texas, in 1983. His story embodies the spirit of innovation and determination. As the third co-founder of Nubank, Edward currently holds 1.98% of the company's equity[128] and has been the driving force behind its technological development and infrastructure.

The search for a co-founder with the expertise to develop Nubank's credit card technology led David to Edward Wible, a Computer Science graduate from Princeton, class of 2005. After completing his studies, Edward joined the Boston Consulting Group (BCG), where he worked in consulting. Two years later, in 2007, he moved to San Francisco to work at Francisco Partners,[129] a leading private equity firm.

In pursuit of new opportunities, Edward transferred to Francisco Partners' London office, where he began to incubate entrepreneurial ideas. Always eager to expand his knowledge, he decided it was time to achieve a long-standing goal: completing a master's degree in business. Taking advantage of his time in Europe, he enrolled at the prestigious INSEAD in France, where he earned his MBA after a year of rigorous study.

---

[128] De Oliveira, Vinicius. UOL. Economia. Dic 2021. "Junqueira, David e Wible: quem são os bilionários fundadores do Nubank".
https://economia.uol.com.br/noticias/redacao/2021/12/21/quem-sao-fundadores-nubank-bilionarios.htm

[129] Francisco Partners Management, L.P., doing business as Francisco Partners, is an American private equity firm, focused exclusively on investments in technology and technology-enabled services businesses. It was founded in August 1999 and is headquartered in San Francisco with offices in London and New York.

Initially, Edward considered France a good place to start a business, but ultimately, it did not convince him. So, he packed his bags and moved to Buenos Aires, with plans to launch a transportation startup. However, this project did not progress as expected, leaving him once again in search of an opportunity that would truly satisfy him.

In a twist of fate, Edward had previously participated in a pilot project with a company where David had served as a board member during his time at Sequoia. During that project, Edward presented so many disruptive ideas that his employers, uninterested in experimenting, felt he was a distraction and eventually decided to let him go. Reflecting on his persistence, Edward once said, *I think I'm a fighter. I like to work hard, keep pushing, continue, and never give up. Just keep going.*[130]

Edward's journey to Nubank began when David traveled directly to Buenos Aires to find him. There, David enthusiastically shared his vision and said, *Cheer up, let's build a bank in Brazil!* The proposal captivated Edward, who felt energized by the prospect of leading the technology for a new financial company.

Edward quickly joined Nubank's founding team. Without hesitation, he flew to São Paulo, arriving with just a small suitcase and a backpack. When they secured the now-famous house on California Street, he settled on the top floor, ready to dive into this new adventure. For many months, he worked nearly 18 hours a day, fully committed to building what would become Nubank.

---

[130] Canaltech. Entrevista Edward Wible. May 2016. "Nubank: o futuro dos cartões de crédito".
https://www.youtube.com/watch?v=UNOlZ2iWg4Y&t=8s

Edward was Nubank's first CTO and literally its first software engineer. In April 2021, he stepped down from the role, passing the torch to Matt Swan, a veteran from Amazon and Booking.com.[131]

Preferring to stay hands-on rather than manage from a corporate level, Edward now leads development teams focused on new systems and infrastructure. He is responsible for innovative technologies at Nubank, including NuSócios, a financial education program aimed at helping millions of Brazilians become investors in the stock market.

Edward played a pivotal role in Nubank's structural design, particularly in its technological development and infrastructure. As CTO, he significantly shaped the way Nubank used innovation to disrupt the banking sector in Brazil. The engineering principles he established at Nubank not only reflected his experience but also embodied the company's core values, always striving for excellence.

In his personal time, Edward is passionate about travel and has visited over 60 countries. He even captained a sailboat for a year, completing a 5,000-nautical-mile journey through Southeast Asia.[132]

---

[131] Booking.com is an online travel company that offers accommodation, transportation and tourist activity booking services. Founded in 1996 in the Netherlands, Booking.com is now one of the leading global platforms in its sector, allowing users to search and book hotels, apartments, hostels, holiday homes and other types of accommodation around the world. The company also provides options for renting cars, booking flights, and finding local activities and attractions. With a wide range of options and a focus on ease of use. Booking makes travel planning and management easier for millions of customers around the world.

[132] SUNO. Perfis. Quem é Edward Wible? https://www.suno.com.br/tudo-sobre/edward-wible/

As Nubank evolved, the engineering area transformed from a culture of implicit principles—similar to an "English constitution," where values were learned through practice—to a more formalized system with clearly written engineering guidelines. This shift came in response to the needs identified as Nubank grew and expanded.

One of Edward's key philosophies was to avoid reliance on a single "process owner" engineer, a common issue with proprietary systems. He believed that processes and systems should belong to the entire company, accessible and understood by all engineers, rather than being controlled by one individual with specialized knowledge. However, as the company grew, maintaining this open culture presented its own challenges. To safeguard Nubank's agility and innovation without succumbing to bureaucracy, Edward and his team developed a set of "engineering principles" in place of rigid rules and regulations.

Nubank's IPO

The Great Leap

Nubank had clear reasons for making its debut on the stock exchange. The first and most obvious was to raise capital on a significant scale—likely the company's last major funding opportunity. This capital was crucial for financing its expansion and developing new products and services, further consolidating its market position.

However, going public was not solely about raising money; it was also a matter of prestige. Listing on the global financial market elevated Nubank's visibility and credibility, placing it in the spotlight for international investors and setting it apart from its competitors.

Additionally, the Initial Public Offering (IPO)[133] provided a golden opportunity for Nubank's early investors and employees to liquidate part of their holdings or, at the very least, see their stakes significantly increase in value as the share price climbed—rewarding their trust and patience in the company's growth.

On December 9, 2021, Nubank reached a monumental milestone by debuting on the New York Stock Exchange (NYSE) under the ticker symbol "NU" and on the São Paulo Stock Exchange (B3) with the ticker "NUBR33." This strategic move

---

[133] IPO is the process by which a private company offers its shares to the public for the first time on a stock exchange. This process allows the company to raise capital from public investors to finance its growth, expand operations, or pay down debt.

marked a new chapter in its evolution, solidifying its status as a disruptive force in the financial sector.

Nubank's journey toward its IPO began on October 27, 2021, when it filed the necessary documentation with the New York Stock Exchange. Aiming to list before the year ended, expectations were high. Nubank sought not only to raise a substantial amount of money but also to seize the perfect moment to capture the financial world's attention and reaffirm its ambition to transform traditional banking.

However, the roadshow[134] revealed a less enthusiastic market reality than expected. Despite underwriters' valuation analyses suggesting a higher share price, investor enthusiasm did not reach the anticipated levels. Analysts seemed to struggle with Nubank's new revenue structure, adhering to the mindset that *if you evaluate a bank, you evaluate it as a bank*—a traditional one, that is. But Nubank was far from a traditional bank.

Nubank's goals were both ambitious and inspiring. The company aimed to raise up to $3.2 billion by selling 289 million shares, with an expected price range of $10 to $11 per share. The target market capitalization[135] was estimated to be around $50 billion.

Under intense pressure from analysts with varying estimates and price targets, Nubank decided to play it safe. The priority was ensuring the success of the IPO. To avoid the risk of

---

[134] *Roadshow*: Before IPO day, company executives hold a "roadshow" or tour to present the company to potential institutional investors and generate interest in the stock offering.

[135] *Market capitalization* is the total market value of a publicly traded company. It is calculated by multiplying your current share price by the total number of shares outstanding.

falling short of expectations, they opted to set the share price between $8 and $9, focusing on achieving their financial objectives without complications.

At the time of the IPO, estimates valued Nubank at approximately $29.3 billion, based on its last funding round, which involved Series G shares (specifically Series G2 and G3). In June 2021, $750 million was raised during this round, including $500 million from Berkshire Hathaway in the G2 series. Any lingering doubts about Nubank being a poor investment were dispelled after the IPO, when Berkshire's NU shares reached a value of $1.278 billion.

When compared to the projected $50 billion valuation for the IPO, these figures highlighted Nubank's extraordinary growth and the high expectations placed on the company. The offering was coordinated by Morgan Stanley, Goldman Sachs, Citigroup, and NuInvest.

In a brilliant move, Edward came up with the idea to offer some of Nubank's Brazilian customers a free Brazilian Depositary Receipt (BDR)[136]. This initiative allowed millions of customers to become shareholders at no cost.

Nubank distributed 20 million BDRs, equivalent to one-sixth of a share, to 7.5 million customers, enabling them to participate in the Brazilian stock market while the shares were traded on the New York Stock Exchange.

When Nubank went public in December 2021, its shares were valued at $9 each. This meant that each BDR was worth approximately $1.50, and customers had to hold these *pedacitos*

---

[136] A BDR is a certificate that represents shares of a foreign company and allows Brazilian investors to participate in foreign stock exchanges.

de NU (little pieces of NU) for at least 12 months before they could trade them. This strategy not only encouraged customer participation in the stock market but also strengthened the bond between Nubank and its broad user base.

On IPO day, David, Cristina, and Edward arrived early in the morning, joined by executives and guests, at the NYSE building for the iconic market opening ceremony. A contingent of about 60 people, all dressed in blue pants and purple jackets with a small NU logo on the chest and "NU / Listed / NYSE" printed in white on the left sleeve, filled the event with Nubank's signature color. The energy was electric, and the festive atmosphere reflected the excitement surrounding this pivotal moment in Nubank's history. It symbolized the company's transition from adolescence to adulthood.

Moments before ringing the bell, David, filled with joy and anticipation, took the opportunity to deliver his final pitch to investors:

> *This IPO will increase our ability to innovate, grow, create new products, and reach more customers.* [137]

The opening bell rang at 9:30 AM, as it does every day, marking the start of the trading session. This time, however, it was NU ringing the bell. Behind the balcony, a massive screen displayed a giant "NU" in white against Nubank's characteristic purple background. The entire NYSE trading floor was decorated

---

[137] Latam Fintech.Forbes Dec 2021. "Nubank empieza a cotizar en la NYSE y se convierte en el banco más valioso de América Latina"
https://www.latamfintech.co/articles/nubank-empieza-a-cotizar-en-la-nyse-y-se-convierte-en-el-banco-cotizado-mas-grande-de-america-latina

in purple, creating a celebratory atmosphere. The balcony was packed with no fewer than 15 people, all beaming with pride, standing shoulder to shoulder as they awaited the moment. At the front, a large golden bell, almost half a meter in diameter, awaited its cue. The honor of ringing the bell went to David, marking a major milestone in Nubank's journey.

Nubank officially made its debut on the New York Stock Exchange, becoming one of the most significant IPOs of the year on Wall Street. With 289 million shares traded, Nubank reached a market capitalization of $48 billion. It opened trading at $11.25 per share—25% above the expected $9. Throughout the day, the stock saw significant activity, with the share price fluctuating before closing at $10.33. By June 2024, less than three years after its IPO, Nubank's stock price had risen to $13.16 per share.

The Influence of Anitta

In June 2021, Nubank made headlines by announcing that Anitta,[138] the renowned Brazilian singer, had joined its board of directors. This decision sparked both interest and controversy. Known for her influence in music and her ability to connect with a wide range of people, Anitta was brought on to assist Nubank with its marketing strategy and the promotion of its financial products, including credit cards and bank accounts.

---

[138] Larissa de Macedo Machado, known professionally as Anitta, is a 31-year-old Brazilian singer, songwriter, dancer, actress and occasional television presenter. She has received numerous accolades, including four Latin American Music Awards and eight Latin Grammy Award nominations. On Instagram she has 65 million followers.

During her time on the board, Anitta made a significant impact. Her extensive experience in marketing and her keen understanding of consumer behavior were invaluable to Nubank as she helped shape and execute campaigns that resonated with a young, tech-savvy audience. In addition to her marketing contributions, Anitta served on the Stakeholders Committee, where she played a key role in advancing the company's ESG (Environmental, Social, and Governance) strategy and the launch of the NU Institute, an initiative dedicated to financial education and inclusion.

Anitta was also heavily involved in the marketing campaigns leading up to Nubank's IPO, using her charisma and strong public connection to generate interest and build trust in the brand. This approach successfully boosted Nubank's visibility while also underscoring its commitment to innovation and inclusion.

In August 2022, Anitta stepped down from the board to assume the role of Global Brand Ambassador for Nubank. In this new capacity, she continues to collaborate closely with the company's marketing teams, lending her strategic vision to help expand the brand both domestically and internationally.

Culture and Values of Nubank

Culture

David has often said:

> ...*culture is the engine. There is nothing more important because culture allows you to hire people; people build products; and products bring you customers.*[139]

Throughout all the challenges David faced while building Nubank, one thing remained very clear to him: Nubank's culture had to be firmly established within the first six months of the company's founding, and it needed to be deeply ingrained in the first 10 to 15 employees. This understanding came from his previous experiences, where he had seen time and again, from the other side of the desk, how different startups operated at General Atlantic and Sequoia.

David's primary concern was how quickly founders must determine what the right culture for their company should be, so

---

[139] Stromeyer, Christopher, Stanford Graduate School of Business. May 2022. Insight by Standford Business. Interview with David. https://www.gsb.stanford.edu/insights/david-velez-position-yourself-scarcity-not-oversupply

that when it starts to take root, it is the correct one. He recognized that a company's culture will always form—either unintentionally or deliberately—and once it takes hold, it is hard to change. As the saying goes, *As the twig is bent, so grows the tree.* A company with a distorted culture is destined for failure.

Corporate culture is the nervous system of a company; it shapes day-to-day operations and guides behavior, even in times of crisis. It consists of the core values and beliefs that drive actions, attitudes, and decisions across all levels, from leadership to every employee. Everyone shares a unified vision and mission that motivates them to work collaboratively toward a common goal. Open and transparent communication is encouraged, ensuring that everyone feels included and valued.

In this work environment, a positive and safe atmosphere is fostered, where good performance is recognized and rewarded. Traditions and events that strengthen team spirit and cohesion are celebrated. The company takes pride in its diversity and strives to be inclusive, valuing the unique experiences and backgrounds of its employees. It remains open to innovation and change, embracing creativity and new ideas that lead to growth and improvement.

When the crisis regarding the shortened payment days for merchants occurred, David saw it as a very serious situation for Nubank—one that could severely damage its credibility with both merchants and the public, something they had worked tirelessly to build. The situation was so critical that NU was on the brink of bankruptcy. David immediately wrestled with whether to communicate this to his employees. On one hand, sharing the news could cause unnecessary anxiety among the staff; on the other hand, nothing had yet happened, so why create alarm?

However, David had always maintained that employees should be treated as owners, a core value at Nubank. He believed in treating them like adults, with full transparency, and keeping them informed about what was happening within the company.

So, when faced with this crisis, David decided to communicate the situation to everyone. Naturally, some employees panicked. But in the end, nothing catastrophic happened. When David arrived at the office that day, he found all the employees proudly wearing their purple T-shirts emblazoned with the slogan, *The Future is Purple*. He gathered them together and explained what had transpired, assuring them that the crisis had been resolved and everything was now under control.

It is precisely in moments like these that company culture is reinforced. Internal trust is strengthened, and transparency is paramount—especially when adversity strikes.

Where Do We Want to Go?

The conclusion was clear: the greatest enemy of the people was complexity, particularly in the financial world, where numerous fees, excessive numbers, limited information, and confusing rules make things difficult. People often become prisoners of this complexity. Therefore, Nubank's cultural mission had to be to combat this complexity and help people.[140]

To preserve this core idea—their DNA—the three founders of Nubank drafted the following values statement:

---

[140] Cfr. Conferencia de David, Universidad de Antioquia. Sep 2023. "Hablemos sobre emprendimiento de alto Impacto".
https://www.youtube.com/live/dxmxUQHAips?si=xc1JBQLOJ4RqcJlB

The company was founded to fight the complexity of the financial system and help people build a truly healthy relationship with their finances.

This mission has guided everything we do, from the creation of innovative products to providing human-centered service, always placing the customer at the heart of our efforts.

(...) Our goal is to revolutionize the way people approach their finances, and we are committed to continuing on this journey.

(...) Together, let us keep shaping the future of finance and making a meaningful difference in people's lives around the world.

Best wishes,
David, Cris, and Ed

Our mission is to fight complexity to empower people. Our motivation is the impact we create in our customers' lives.[141]

To ensure this foundational idea, their DNA, was not lost, the three founders of Nubank drafted the following statement of values:[142]

---

[141] Ibidem. Código de Conducta de Nubank.
[142] Código de Ética de Nubank.
https://cdn.nubank.com.br/MX/codigo-de-conducta.pdf

This same culture of *being there for the customer* drives Nubank to continuously offer more and better products to its clients.

One idea that deeply resonated with David during his time at Sequoia was the importance of establishing Nubank's culture within the first six months—*beginning with the first 10 to 15 employees. These individuals would form the foundation for the company's next 30 years.*

They sought out people *who asked questions, not those who came with their minds full of fixed answers.* They wanted individuals who were open to understanding, diverse in their perspectives, eager to participate, and willing to choose the best solution rather than simply defending their own.

This emphasis on culture is so important to David Vélez that he personally takes the time to explain it to every employee, especially new hires, ensuring they hear Nubank's values directly from him. He outlines the "rituals" and practices that help keep these values alive. Nubank, in turn, has documented these aspects, creating recordings of employees who explain the company's collaborative approach and way of working.

At its core, David explains that people want to engage with those who treat them well, who provide good service at a fair price. They do not want to deal with institutions that treat them poorly.

Values

At the core of Nubank lies a vibrant and bold philosophy that guides every action—a true Revolutionary Culture. This mindset, distilled into five fundamental principles, has allowed the company to redefine the banking sector in Latin America, turning every step into a statement of its mission.

These are its five guiding principles:

A. We want our customers to love us fanatically.
We believe that delighting customers is essential to building strong, long-term relationships based on loyalty and trust.

B. We are hungry and challenge the status quo.
We encourage our teams never to settle for how things have always been done, but instead to question and push boundaries.

C. We build strong and diverse teams.
We are committed to assembling teams with the best talent, regardless of their background, characteristics, or experience, bringing diverse perspectives into the fold.

D. We act as owners, not tenants.
We treat our employees as partners, fostering relationships grounded in humility, respect, transparency, and accountability. Our culture is entirely focused on serving our customers, with no place for ego or status symbols. Mistakes are embraced as opportunities for learning and growth.

E. **We pursue smart efficiency.**
We build scalable systems and optimize the use of all resources: our teams, time, and capital. As we gain efficiency, we pass these gains on to our customers through lower rates and fees.

Nubank seeks not only to satisfy its customers but to turn them into true fans. Customer satisfaction is the cornerstone of its strategy, creating relationships based on loyalty and trust. This obsession with the customer translates into exceptional service that not only meets expectations but consistently exceeds them.

The hunger for innovation is another essential pillar. Nubank fosters a culture that challenges the status quo. Here, no team settles for traditional methods; every employee is encouraged to question, experiment, and find new ways to improve. This constant drive toward innovation keeps Nubank at the forefront of a sector known for its resistance to change.

Diversity and inclusion are not mere goals but active realities, truly a source of creativity precisely because of the diversity of experiences, professions, ages, and genders. Nubank works tirelessly to form teams composed of the best talents, regardless of their professional backgrounds. This diversity enriches creativity and strengthens the team, ensuring more inclusive and effective solutions.

As we have mentioned, at Nubank, employees are treated as partners. Relationships are based on humility, respect, transparency, and accountability. This approach eliminates selfishness and status symbols, fostering an environment where mistakes are opportunities for learning and growth.

Smart efficiency is another key principle. Nubank seeks not only to do more with less but to do it more intelligently. They build scalable systems and optimize all resources: teams, time, and capital. Efficiency gains are directly passed on to customers, reducing rates and fees.

Vision and Mission

Since its founding, Nubank's vision has been clear: *to democratize financial services*. The founders, driven by their passion for emerging markets and the digitalization of banking, have worked tirelessly to make banking more accessible, affordable, and customer-friendly for millions of people across Latin America. Their goal is to eliminate excessive fees and unnecessary bureaucracy.

From the outset, David implemented a disruptive strategy rooted in digital technology. This approach has enabled Nubank to optimize every aspect of banking, reducing costs while significantly enhancing the customer experience.

Nubank's unshakable philosophy of *customer first* serves as a foundational pillar. Every decision is made with the customer's convenience and satisfaction as the top priority, ensuring their needs are always front and center. This blend of strong principles and a clear vision has fueled Nubank's exponential growth and redefined what it means to be a bank in the 21st century.

The NU Brand

The story of Nubank is not only told through its financial achievements and innovative technology but also through its visual identity. A key moment came when Doug Leone recommended changing the company's original name, EOS.

David, always open to improvement, set out to find a name that better captured the company's mission and vision. From this effort, Nubank was born.

The task of creating this new identity was entrusted to Garupa Design, a Brazilian design studio founded by Gustavo Duarte. Their goal was to design a brand that was modern, innovative, and accessible—perfectly aligned with Nubank's mission to transform banking.

The choice of purple and the design of the logo were not random. They were strategically selected to stand out from traditional banks, which typically used conservative colors like blue and gray. Purple symbolized a fresh, disruptive alternative in the financial sector.

The designers explain:

> *True to its original intent, the Nubank brand evokes a sense of joy and simplicity. The name 'NU' is more than just a clever play on words; in Portuguese, it means 'naked,' symbolizing transparency and honesty.*

Nubank's Visual Renewal

In 2021, Nubank continued its evolution, this time unveiling a new logo.

The curves that form the 'NU' are now softer and more rounded, reflecting our human side. The design's fluidity has also changed; it resembles two twisting ribbons, symbolizing a continuous movement—just as we are always evolving. The colors now give more weight to the letters, making the text more accessible and representing the maturity of our products. Above all, this transformation conveys our most important value: closeness to people.[143]

To update the brand identity, the company collaborated closely with Pentagram partners Eddie Opara and Marina Willer and their teams in London and New York—the same design firm behind MasterCard's new logo.[144]

Nubank's new brand identity marks a significant shift from its previous image, dropping the word "bank" to better align with its vision of redefining banking and business.[145]

While the new identity maintains Nubank's signature purple—famous for the "roxinho" (little purple) cards—it also

---

[143] Cfr. Nubank Editorial. https://building.nubank.com.br/new-logo-nubank/
[144] Fernández, Laura. Graffica. Branding. Jul 2016. "El rediseño de MasterCard. Simplicidad y conectividad". https://graffica.info/el-rediseno-de-MasterCard/
[145] Pentagram, Nubank, Identidad de Marca. https://www.pentagram.com/work/nubank/story

broadens the color palette to make it versatile across different sectors and audiences.

Nubank Fans

Different Types of Customers

Buying a cellphone or a television is straightforward: you select the product, pay for it, and take it home. If you are dissatisfied, you can simply avoid that brand in the future and share your negative experience with others. You might even return the item, and that is the end of it. In this type of transaction, the process is quick, and the value of the product is immediate and tangible.

Financial services, however, are more complex and involve ongoing interaction. Whether you are opening an account or applying for a loan, you enter into a continuous relationship with the bank. This relationship requires trust and good service because you are entrusting the institution with your money and financial future.

While customer service for physical products emphasizes efficiency and speed, customer service for financial services demands ongoing attention, reliability, and a high level of personalization to build and maintain the client's trust.

Nubank Customers

In an interview, David reflected on one of the most critical aspects of any company: customer retention.

It is simple but clear. People want to be with people who treat them well, and customers want to be with institutions that treat them well. [146]

To develop Nubank's approach to customer service, David and his co-founders spent considerable time studying companies renowned for their exceptional customer experience management. For instance, they spent two days with Zappos,[147] learning how the company operates and structures its organization. They did the same with Disney,[148] Southwest Airlines, and Amazon. The topic of customer experience deeply fascinated them. Nubank even sent employees to Disney for specialized training in delivering that magical customer experience. Ultimately, however, Nubank discovered its own unique formula.

---

[146] Cfr. Op.Cit. Trava, Oswaldo. Abr 2020. Podcast Nubank.

[147] Zappos is an online retail company known primarily for its wide selection of footwear. Founded in 1999, Zappos has stood out for its focus on customer service and unique business culture. It offers a variety of products including clothing, accessories and more. In 2009, Zappos was acquired by Amazon. The company is recognized for its easy return policy and exceptional customer service, which has contributed to its popularity and success in the electronic commerce market.

[148] Disney Institute is dedicated to offering training and consultancy to external companies and professionals. They teach commercial practices and leadership principles based on Disney strategies and success. Offers seminars, workshops, and personalized programs in areas such as leadership, organizational culture, customer service, and innovation. These programs are based on the methods and philosophies that have made Disney successful.

As of the time of this writing, Nubank has reached the significant milestone of 100 million customers—a figure that, in a world where astronomical numbers are commonplace, might not initially stand out. Yet in the banking sector, it is monumental. Only three banks globally can claim a larger customer base, and all of them are in China. For instance, the Industrial and Commercial Bank of China has over 700 million customers. Outside of China, however, Nubank leads the pack with 100 million customers, followed by BBVA with 70 million, Bank of America with 68 million, and JPMorgan Chase with 60 million.[149]

Reaching this milestone is extraordinary for Nubank, especially considering they achieved it in just 11 years. All of Nubank's efforts are focused on capturing the largest possible market share—in essence, attracting customers.

Interestingly, despite being known for its youthful, millennial, and unconventional image, Nubank has managed to attract 50% of Brazil's senior adult population as customers. Yet, despite this achievement, their overall market share is not as large as one might assume.

David reflected on this substantial portion of Brazil's adult population:

> Yes, that is how vast the opportunity we have in front of us is! Not even JPMorgan can claim something similar in the United States!

---

[149] Cfr. Jimenea, Adrian, et al. Abr. 2024. S&P Global. "The world's largest banks by assets, 2024".
https://www.spglobal.com/marketintelligence/en/news-insights/research/the-worlds-largest-banks-by-assets-2024

This is an enormous customer base that has entrusted Nubank with their savings and confidence, making the company one of the most valuable and trusted brands in Brazil and across Latin America.

At Nubank, everything truly revolves around the customer. Cristina remarked:

> *We must never assume that the customer is here to stay. Every day, we need to continue earning their loyalty, because they can leave at any moment. They have to choose to stay with us. We did not want to lock them in with tricks or contracts. We want them to want to be here with us, to choose us, to love us. I think that is the real secret.* [150]

Customer Service

Nubank believes its distinction from other financial institutions lies in its relentless commitment to continuous improvement. Many customers complaints stem from things not working as expected, prompting them to seek help. At Nubank, the guiding principle is to make this happen less and less, and the key to achieving that is automating as much as possible—so the app can handle everything smoothly. If an error occurs, a question arises, or something does not function as it should, they are dedicated to resolving it immediately. It is ingrained in their culture. They firmly believe that this approach will set them apart

---

[150] InvestNews BR. May 2023. "Nubank mira em alta renda e Inteligência Artificial, diz Cris Junqueira".
https://www.youtube.com/watch?v=b2q9BXkXkcQ

in the industry, especially since many companies tend to stop actively pursuing solutions after reaching a certain point.

For many institutions, it is enough to hand everything over to the call center to sort out the issue, and once the problem is untangled, they consider it resolved. But Nubank continually strives to go beyond this. For them, being *close enough* to the customer is not sufficient. Their goal is to improve continuously, solve problems at the root, and bring greater efficiency to every interaction. That is their mission and what they aim to achieve.

The Xpeers

Talking to Nubank's customer service is a surprisingly pleasant experience. They respond in a very informal, friendly manner while efficiently resolving your issue. The people who work in customer service at Nubank have a very different profile compared to those typically hired by traditional banks. Nubank calls them Xpeers, and they are dedicated exclusively to customer service. Their role is to assist customers, answer questions, solve problems, and fully understand the situation. They serve as the bridge between the customers and the bank. This large, diverse team is made up of over 25 different nationalities, allowing them to provide support in multiple languages, including Portuguese, Spanish, English, French, and Italian.

Cristina once shared a telling anecdote about how the Xpeers operate. One day, a customer called customer service, excitedly requesting an increase to his credit card limit. His excitement stemmed from a very special reason: he wanted to buy a ring to propose to his girlfriend.

The Xpeer who helped him not only approved the limit increase but was also moved by the customer's story. Displaying an uncommon level of empathy and care, he decided to follow the outcome of this important moment. The story soon reached other team members, who later received a photo of the couple. Without hesitation, they printed and framed the photo. Shortly after, they sent the framed picture to the customer's address, creating a lasting keepsake of that unique moment.[151]

As we often hear, customers should be treated not as mere numbers but as individuals with their own stories and dreams. While that sounds admirable, putting it into practice is another challenge altogether.

This customer service philosophy is so fundamental to Nubank that, in September 2017, they decided to create an annual event where everyone—from analysts to directors—would participate as Xpeers. During this event, even the founders got involved: Cristina Junqueira, Edward Wible, and David Vélez each took four-hour shifts to engage directly with customers.

Edward, despite grappling with the challenging northeastern Brazilian accent, managed to handle around 25 calls. David, with his characteristic enthusiasm and dedication, responded to about 30 calls. Cristina, always committed, also attended to a substantial number of customer inquiries.[152]

---

[151] De Nuccio, Dony. InvestNews BR. May 2023. "Nubank mira em alta renda e Inteligencia Artificial diz Cris Junqueira".
https://youtu.be/b2q9BXkXkcQ?si=l-t-GCjctnRcQI62
[152] NZN. The Brief. Sep 2017. "O CEO do Nubank senta na cadeira do SAC"
https://www.youtube.com/watch?v=w0cwc99WcDw

This initiative was specifically designed to inspire the entire team to stay focused on providing excellent service and fostering empathy.[153]

The vision behind the Xpeers concept is even more ambitious: the customer service team includes not only customer service professionals but also application engineers. The aim is not just to assist customers, but to give engineers firsthand insight into the issues that arise in their systems. The idea was for engineers to hear directly from customers about what they were experiencing and what was not working in the app. This approach ensures that both the Xpeers and the engineering teams have a clearer understanding of how to collaborate and resolve problems together.

What was particularly interesting was the emphasis on understanding both the frustrations and the excitement of customers. David noted that it is very easy for engineers or directors to forget how frustrating it can be for customers when something in the system does not work properly. This initiative offered a valuable opportunity to genuinely understand and serve customers in the way they want to be served.

Through this, Nubank not only commits to providing solutions but ensures that every team member, regardless of their role, understands the significance of the customer experience. This collaborative and empathetic approach has not only improved service but also strengthened the relationship with users, ensuring they feel heard and valued in every interaction. Nubank's culture is young, informal, and rooted in honesty. The guiding principle is to treat customers like friends, The guiding principle is to treat customers like friends, eliminating the

---

[153] Cfr. NZN. The Brief. Sep 2017.

formality of *you and us*, a common convention in business environments that typically establishes a structured and formal relationship between its clients and the company. Instead, Nubank fosters a more personal connection. The team is well-compensated to ensure high-quality service, as Nubank views customer service not merely as an obligation, but as a priority to deliver the best care possible.[154]

The ultimate goal is to solve problems, not just listen and log them into a system. Nubank focuses on truly understanding the issue and finding solutions, avoiding technical jargon that might confuse customers. The premise is that 99.9% of problems can be resolved, always seeking the easiest and most cost-effective solution in terms of time and resources.

They have systems that provide real-time information and a process to capture customer feedback on service and product performance. During a call, both teams are involved: one directly assists the customer, while the systems team listens to the issues. This collaboration helps engineers make necessary adjustments to improve functionality by identifying patterns and addressing them.

To train Xpeers, Nubank heavily relies on mentoring by more experienced employees, teaching the right tone of voice, communication style, and customer service approach. While they do have documentation and manuals, the guiding philosophy remains: *Treat customers as you would like to be treated.*

---

[154] Canaltech. Entrevista Edward Wible. May 2016. "Nubank: o futuro dos cartões de crédito".
https://www.youtube.com/watch?v=UNOIZ2iWg4Y&t=8s

David commented on the event: *It is not too much to ask that everyone, at least once a year, spends a day listening to customers; it brings us closer to them and helps us stay focused.*

So far, Nubank has chosen to prioritize 100% human service rather than relying on automated bots. *It is a huge responsibility because we are dealing with customers' money, and we take that very seriously,"* affirmed Edward.[155]

A striking example of the effectiveness of this strategy is reflected in the testimony of a Nubank customer who said, *If I have to choose which card to pay first, I always choose Nubank because it is the only one that has treated me well.*

This simple yet powerful statement captures the essence of the relationship Nubank has built with its customers. It is not just about offering a financial product; it is about providing a humane and empathetic experience. This emotional connection and the feeling of being valued drive customers to prioritize Nubank over its competitors

Marketing Campaigns

A marketing campaign is not just a collection of scattered activities; it is a carefully orchestrated series of tactics designed to promote a product, service, or brand and achieve specific objectives within a defined timeframe. Its effectiveness depends on thorough market research and a deep understanding of the target audience. A successful campaign employs a cohesive mix

---

[155] NZN. The Brief. Ed Wible. "O que o CTO da Nubank pensa sobre atendimento ao cliente" https://www.youtube.com/watch?v=uUJ-t7qsQaQ

of communication channels and tools, such as advertising, public relations, digital marketing, and promotions. The true measure of success lies in its ability to build brand recognition, attract and retain customers, and ultimately drive sales and company growth. Its core mission is to make the product known to both future and current customers.

By this logic, a revolutionary product like Nubank should have required a massive marketing campaign to gain visibility, especially in a market crowded with competitors. However, reality presented challenges that radically altered Nubank's original plans.

When Nubank was ready to launch its credit card, the logical approach was to promote it aggressively with a big campaign. Yet, the very nature of credit cards made this task more complicated, and David's cautious approach, mindful of the significant risks involved, led to a different strategy.

Nubank first needed to deeply understand its customers because, with a credit card, they were essentially lending money, expecting to be repaid while earning a commission on each transaction. Given this, launching a massive promotion was not an option, as their risk analysis system still required fine-tuning.

It was not the right time for a high-cost, wide-reaching campaign. Instead, they needed to gradually introduce the card to the public, perhaps in a simple and low-profile way. David decided on a more subtle and targeted approach: getting a magazine to feature them, aiming to generate curiosity and attract potential customers. Although the first mention did not have the desired impact, a second appearance in a specialized magazine, some time later, successfully captured consumer attention. This sparked an avalanche of applications, leading to exponential growth in demand for their cards.

However, this success created a new problem that intensified daily: Nubank could not serve all the applicants at once. They needed to slow things down, as they could only process 15 to 20% of the applications. Clearly, a marketing campaign was no longer a priority. Instead, they adopted a new strategy: rather than actively driving demand, they allowed applications to come in naturally without immediately approving them, preventing their system from becoming overloaded until it was fully optimized.

However, Nubank still needed to respond to everyone who had applied for the card. To address this, they ingeniously implemented a waitlist, which reassured applicants while also helping to build a large base of future customers. Unexpectedly, this waitlist generated even more demand by creating a sense of scarcity. In line with basic economic principles, people began to desire the card even more because it was so difficult to obtain.

As a result, the need for a large marketing campaign diminished. Nubank realized they no longer needed to invest heavily in traditional marketing efforts. This unexpected shift allowed the company to redefine its strategy, focusing on value-driven and cultural marketing. In doing so, they solidified their unique identity and strengthened their relationship with customers.

Customer Acquisition Cost

In any company, Customer Acquisition Cost (CAC) is a critical metric for assessing the efficiency of marketing and sales strategies. This indicator reflects the total cost of attracting a new customer, including expenses for advertising, promotions, and sales efforts. Effectively managing CAC enables companies to optimize their resources, identify the most effective marketing channels, and maximize return on investment (ROI).[156]

CAC is calculated by dividing the total marketing and sales expenses by the number of new customers acquired during a specific period.

Nubank's CAC

At Nubank, the Customer Acquisition Cost (CAC) is remarkably low. According to the latest data from the first quarter of 2024, the cost to acquire a new customer was just $7, with $2 of that spent on paid advertising.

This is significantly lower compared to the average CAC in the financial industry, which ranged between $146 and $173 as of September 2023.[157] According to Nubank, their acquisition cost is 85% lower than that of their competitors. This "low" CAC not only reflects the efficiency of Nubank's strategies but also provides them with a significant competitive advantage in the financial market.

Another crucial metric is their Customer Service Cost. Nubank reports that their average service cost is less than $1 per

---

[156] The ROI (Return on Investment) is a financial metric that measures the profitability of an investment. It is calculated by dividing the net benefit of the investment between the cost of the investment and expressed as a percentage. ROI allows companies to evaluate the efficiency of an investment or compare the profitability of several investments

[157] Cfr. FisrtPageSage. Sep 2023. "Average Customer Acquisition Cost (CAC) By Industry" https://firstpagesage.com/reports/average-cac-by-industry-b2c-edition/

active customer, which is also approximately 85% lower than traditional or incumbent banks.

A key driver of customer acquisition for Nubank is its own users. From the early days of the famous waitlist for credit cards to today, most of Nubank's new customers come through word-of-mouth recommendations.

This phenomenon is no accident; it is the result of a carefully crafted strategy that transforms every customer into a brand ambassador. The satisfaction and loyalty of Nubank's users lead to enthusiastic recommendations to friends, family, and colleagues. This organic dynamic has been, and continues to be, one of the strongest pillars of Nubank's exponential growth.

Organic Marketing

In word-of-mouth marketing, each positive experience becomes a shared story, creating a network of trust and credibility that extends far beyond the reach of traditional marketing. This approach not only reduces customer acquisition costs but also strengthens relationships with existing users, fostering loyalty and promoting sustainable, efficient growth.

Nubank's success in maintaining a low CAC while ensuring high customer satisfaction highlights the effectiveness of its marketing and customer service strategies. By prioritizing exceptional experiences and personalized service, Nubank attracts new customers and keeps them engaged and loyal, driving continuous growth and securing a strong foothold in the financial market.

Net Promoter Score

At Nubank, the Net Promoter Score (NPS) serves as a guiding compass, with everything revolving around their customers. The idea is simple: customers are the stars of the show, and measuring their satisfaction is crucial.

While the NPS is a standout metric on its own, another indicator is even more telling: daily customer growth. Together, these two metrics are like the pulse and breath of Nubank, offering a real-time view of the company's overall health.

The NPS

The NPS, that customer loyalty gauge, was devised by Fred Reichheld in 2006 and presented in his book *The Ultimate Question*. Today, it's the favorite thermometer of many companies to assess customer satisfaction and predict business growth.

And how is this indicator calculated?

The process is as simple as asking, listening, and categorizing. It revolves around asking customers a single question, resulting in a number between -100 and 100.

The question could be something like:

> *On a scale of 0 to 10, how likely are you to recommend our company/product/service to a friend or colleague?*

The responses are divided into three groups:

Promoters (score 9-10): These are the die-hard fans, the loyal and enthusiastic customers who will keep buying and shout your name from the rooftops.

Passives (score 7-8): They're happy, yes, but not entirely thrilled. They're like those friends who appreciate you but won't hesitate to change plans if they find something better.

Detractors (score 0-6): Here's the critical group. These dissatisfied customers can make a lot of negative noise, damaging the brand's reputation with their harsh critiques.

Thus, with just one question, Nubank can measure the heartbeat and oxygenation of its business, ensuring that each day is better than the last.

Having the customer response numbers, the metric is then calculated.

Calculating the NPS:

From the percentage of Promoters, we must subtract the percentage of Detractors.

NPS = % Promoters - % Detractors

The result will be a number ranging from -100 to 100.

A **Positive NPS (>0)** indicates that most customers are Promoters and are satisfied with the company.

A **Negative NPS (<0)** suggests more Detractors than Promoters, indicating that many customers are dissatisfied.

A **Neutral NPS (0)** means there are equal numbers of Promoters and Detractors.

Nubank's global NPS is +90.[158]

The NPS is a valuable tool because:

- It is easy to understand and implement.
- It enables companies to benchmark themselves against competitors and track their own progress over time.
- It helps prioritize customer experience and improving loyalty.
- A high NPS typically correlates with greater growth and future profitability.

However, the NPS has its limitations. It is one-dimensional and does not provide detailed insights into the reasons behind the scores. Since it relies on a single question, careful phrasing is essential.

Additionally, responses can vary significantly across different cultures and countries and may be influenced by external factors beyond the company's control.

---

[158] Novene, Chloe. Startupeable. Dic 2021. Nubank IPO: Las Métricas detrás de su salida a la Bolsa". https://startupeable.com/nubank-ipo/#:~:text=Nubank%20tiene%20un%20NPS%20%2B90,%2C%20especialmente%2C%20en%20servicios%20financieros.

David asked the question:[159]

What is the highest NPS? Surprisingly, it is not Tesla, nor the iPhone. The highest and best NPS of any consumer product in the world, across all categories, belongs to our purple credit card in Mexico, with a score of 94—the highest in the entire banking industry worldwide.

Nubank's NPS in Brazil is 88,[160] which is truly remarkable. An NPS above 70 is considered world-class in terms of customer loyalty and satisfaction. For context, QuestionPro, a company that tracks NPS across various industries, reports that the average NPS in the financial industry is 34. The industry with the highest NPS, Education and Training, reaches a maximum of 71.

For Nubank to achieve an NPS of +90 is extraordinary. This feat is even more impressive considering Nubank operates within the financial sector, which traditionally suffers from a poor reputation—a point David has often emphasized.

In Mexico, the average NPS in the financial services industry was 28 in 2018, rising slightly to 32 in 2019. Nubank's credit card received a score of 94 in the second quarter of 2021, and by August 2022, that score had increased to 96.[161]

---

[159] Cfr. Stebbings, Harry. Entrevista 20VC. E1059. Sep 2023. "David Velez: How AI Changes The Future of Finance".
https://youtu.be/as_jwvokTDI?si=BYdjebgg28wLZoRQ
[160] Cfr. Op. Cit. Knox, Fortt. Entrevista. Ago 2023.
[161] NU. Redacción. "Nu México: Una financiera sólida y regulada".
https://blog.nu.com.mx/net-promoter-score-de-nu-amamos-saber-que-piensan-nuestros-clientes/

This success is largely attributed to several key strategies at Nubank. One standout factor is their investment in customer service. While marketing expenses accounted for roughly 10% of Nubank's operating expenses in 2019, customer service and operations made up around 30%, with a significant portion dedicated to the call center.

This demonstrates that, despite being a digital bank, people still highly value the ability to speak with real individuals and access support when they need it.

Product Innovation

With the goal of eliminating the complexities and costs associated with traditional banks, Nubank began by developing a simple yet powerful product: a credit card with no annual fees, managed entirely through a mobile app.

The card was launched in the Brazilian market in 2014, following an intense development phase during which the team focused on creating a user-friendly interface that made managing financial operations as easy as possible for customers.

Nubank was born as a single, 100% mobile application, initially operating on iOS and Android, even before a web version was available.[162] This made Nubank a true mobile banking solution, specifically designed for smartphones. Additionally, from day one, Nubank operated as a fully cloud-based bank, avoiding the need to build its own data center. This allowed them access to the latest and most advanced software at low cost and, in some cases, even for free, eliminating the need for expensive software licenses.

Nubank demonstrated remarkable efficiency; since the product launch and the issuance of the first cards, they had spent less than a million dollars of their initial capital.

Building on their early success with credit cards, Nubank continued to expand its product portfolio, always prioritizing simplicity and user experience. Every new product was designed to address common challenges faced by traditional bank

---

[162] Cfr. International Finance Corporation. Latin Focus. Nov 2023. Entrevista a Cristina Junqueiras. https://www.youtube.com/watch?v=G3zjje7jx1k

customers, making financial management easier and more accessible.

Nubank's First Product

On April 1, 2014, Nubank made its first financial transaction with a product that would revolutionize the financial sector: the Nubank Mastercard purple credit card—a simple yet highly disruptive product for the global financial market.

Traditionally, banks typically offer savings accounts as their first product to new customers. However, Nubank took a different approach: they launched with a credit card. This decision was driven by regulatory and strategic factors—and, quite frankly, because there were few other options available.

By law, in nearly every country, only financial institutions with express authorization from the authorities can accept deposits from consumers. In Nubank's case, obtaining a banking license from the Central Bank of Brazil, which would have allowed them to accept deposits, seemed like a daunting task. They were warned that the process could take years, and on top of that, foreigners were prohibited from operating banks. As a result, the most practical solution was to offer a credit card, which required permission to operate as a Payment Institution—allowing Nubank to enter the market.

What initially seemed like an obstacle turned out to be a fortunate turn of events. It pushed Nubank to completely reinvent the concept of the credit card, catching traditional financial institutions off guard. Nubank focused on delivering an innovative and accessible product, managed entirely through a mobile app, which not only shifted the financial sector's paradigms but also set new industry standards.

On the other hand, and equally important, launching with a deposit or savings account when no one knows you makes it much more difficult to gain immediate trust. Convincing people to entrust you with their money is undoubtedly a more challenging task.

The key difference is that when lending money, you do not need to have 100% of your customers' trust—because you are the one trusting them. You are the one taking the risk by lending them money. This meant that Nubank had to be extremely cautious in deciding whom to lend to and how much, a task that was certainly complex.

From the consumer's perspective, David noted that it was a way to *start a conversation with them, let them try the product, and introduce them to a new brand.* Additionally, Nubank's credit card offered many appealing features: no fees or charges of any kind, except for interest on purchases the customer chose to defer. If they paid off the balance in full at the end of the cycle, they paid absolutely nothing.

The credit card, a universally familiar product, became the perfect Trojan horse for Nubank—a way to enter the financial system through the front door without traditional banks even noticing. It was a direct way to show that Nubank was here to address consumers' most pressing financial challenges.

The Credit Card

Since its invention, the credit card has been one of the most profitable products in a bank's portfolio.

Over the nearly 70 years that credit cards have existed, banks have added a series of "improvements" that have turned them into sophisticated tools for trapping consumers in long-term debt. Cristina, in an interview with *Forbes*, commented specifically on credit cards:

> *If banks are Darth Vader, credit cards are the Death Star. It's the horrible weapon banks have used for years.*[163]

Recalling her years working with a renowned Brazilian bank, she said:

> *I never really understood why we had to shove these horrible products with high rates down people's throats through very aggressive telemarketing. Customers hated it.*[164]

---

[163] Forbes. Entrevista con Cristina Junqueira. May 2024. https://www.forbes.com/profile/Cristina-junqueira/?sh=1258924c8d9d
[164] Cfr. Forbes. Entrevista con Cristina Junqueira. May 2024

Caveat Emptor

All credit cards, when handed to the consumer, should come with a clear label that reads *Caveat Emptor*[165] –Consumer Beware!– warning customers that "**Incorrect use of this instrument can cause serious and severe financial problems.**"

The origin of credit cards dates back to the 1920s, though it was not until 1946 that the Flatbush National Bank of Brooklyn introduced the first official credit card, known as "Charge-It."[166] This program was run in partnership with select bank customers and various local businesses. At the end of an agreed period, the businesses would bring their sales tickets to the bank, and the bank would collect the payments from their customers.

Credit cards quickly gained popularity, especially after Frank McNamara[167] introduced a more universal card, the Diners Club, in 1950. This card was intended for use in restaurants. The idea came to McNamara after he found himself in an awkward situation at a restaurant, realizing he did not have enough money to pay the bill, so his wife had to go home to get it. The concept took off rapidly, leading to competition from others, such as the

---

[165] The Latin phrase "Caveat Emptor," which translates as "let the buyer beware" or "buyer beware." This expression is used in law and business to indicate that the buyer is responsible for checking the quality and suitability of goods before purchasing them, and that, in general, they cannot complain after purchase if the product turns out to be defective, unless that there is fraud or an explicit guarantee.

[166] Murray, Christopher, Bankrate, Dec 2022. "The history of credit cards". https://www.bankrate.com/credit-cards/news/the-evolution-of-credit-cards/

[167] Cfr. Bellis, Mary. Thought Co. History & Culture. Feb 2019. "Invention of Credit Cards". https://www.thoughtco.com/who-invented-credit-cards-1991484

American Express card and Bank of America's BankAmericard, which would later become VISA.[168]

Initially, credit cards were marketed as a convenience, especially for traveling salespeople who had to sell across the U.S., reducing the need to carry cash and making transactions easier. The model was the same as it is today: *money is lent, and if not paid on time, interest is charged*. However, the rapid growth in usage and intense competition among banks led to abusive practices and a lack of transparency that ultimately harmed consumers.

These practices included exorbitant interest rates, hidden fees, and unclear terms and conditions that trapped consumers in a cycle of growing debt, both principal and interest. The lack of transparency and unfair conditions left many users in precarious financial situations, eroding trust in financial institutions and increasing the demand for a fairer, more transparent alternative.

The rapid expansion of credit card use created a significant multiplier effect on consumer debt.[169] Many people found themselves in financial trouble due to the ease of obtaining credit and the lack of regulation on rates, fees, and credit management practices.[170] This issue worsened in the 1960s and

---

[168] Visa. Historia de Visa. https://corporate.visa.com/en
[169] Durkin, Thomas A. Reserva Federal de los EE. UU. "Credit Cards: Use and Consumer Attitudes, 1970–2000"
https://www.federalreserve.gov/pubs/bulletin/2000/0900lead.pdf#:~:text=URL%3A%20https%3A%2F%2Fwww.federalreserve.gov%2Fpubs%2Fbulletin%2F2000%2F0900lead.pdf%0AVisible%3A%200%25%20
[170] Drozd, Lukasz. Artículo. Federal Reserve Bank of Philadelphia. 2021. "Why Credit Cards Played a Surprisingly Big Role in the Great Recession" https://www.philadelphiafed.org/-/media/frbp/assets/economy/articles/economic-insights/2021/q2/eiq221-credit-cards-and-the-great-

1970s, prompting the U.S. Congress to intervene with legislation such as the Truth in Lending Act of 1968 and the Fair Debt Collection Practices Act of 1977.

However, not all regulations favored consumers. In 1996, the Supreme Court's decision in *Smiley vs. Citibank*[171] allowed banks to charge late fees nationwide, regardless of state laws. This deregulation enabled credit card companies to impose higher interest rates, exacerbating the growing debt problem.[172]

By 2017, approximately 192 million Americans —76% of the population over 18—[173] owned some form of credit card,[174] with an average of 3.7 active cards per person.[175] This contributed to massive debt, with credit card debt collectively reaching a trillion dollars.[176]

To make matters worse, competition among banks led to the creation of cards with even more exclusive features, often implying higher fees for these "privileges."

---

recession.pdf#:~:text=URL%3A%20https%3A%2F%2F www.philadelphiafed.org%2F

[171] Caso "Smiley v. Citibank (South Dakota), N. A.".
https://en.wikipedia.org/wiki/Smiley_v._Citibank_(South_Dakota),_N._A

[172] Oyez. Hechos del Caso. 1996. "Smiley v. Citibank (South Dakota), N. A.".
https://www.oyez.org/cases/1995/95-860

[173] Census Gov. 2017.
https://www.census.gov/quickfacts/table/PST045216/00

[174] McCann, Adam. WalletHub. May 2024. "Number of Credit Cards and Credit Card Holders".
https://wallethub.com/edu/cc/number-of-credit-cards/25532/

[175] Daly, Lyle. The Ascent. May 2024. "How many Credit Cards Should I Have?" https://www.fool.com/the-ascent/credit-cards/articles/how-many-credit-cards-does-the-average-person-have/

[176] Federal Reserve System. May 2024. "Consumer Credit G.19".
https://www.federalreserve.gov/releases/g19/current/

While credit cards started as a financial convenience, their evolution led to significant debt and fostered abusive practices that posed serious risks to consumers. The ease of access to credit, combined with insufficient regulation, has created a widespread problem not only in the United States but also across the globe.

A Tale of Innovation and Prudence

Imagine, for a moment, the vast number of credit cards in circulation in the United States. The top ten issuers control nearly 90% of the market, with around 572 million credit cards in use. When debit and store cards are included, that number exceeds 1.6 billion cards.[177] In 2023, the average balance on a bank-issue credit card was $6,360.[178]

To put this into perspective, in Mexico, according to the information from the National Banking and Securities Commission (CNBV), at the end of 2023, there were 37.8 million credit cards in circulation by the end of 2023.[179]

---

[177] Thangavelu, Poonkulali. Bankrate. Jul 2023. "Credit card market share statistics".https://www.bankrate.com/credit-cards/news/credit-card-market-share-statistics/
[178] Pokora, Becky. Forbes Advisor. Mar 2024. "Credit Card Statistics". https://www.forbes.com/advisor/credit-cards/credit-card-statistics/#how_many_credit_cards_do_americans_have_section
[179] Banco de México. Sistema de Información Económica. Dic. 2023. "Número de tarjetas de crédito y débito - (CF256)" https://www.banxico.org.mx/SieInternet/consultarDirectorioInternetAction.do?accion=consultarCuadro&idCuadro=CF256&sector=5&locale=es

Some banks have sought to make their cards more exclusive by changing the materials used—introducing metal cards as a luxury differentiator, ranging from aluminum to titanium. Today, there are over 20 types of metal cards, adding an extra layer of prestige to the "Black," "Sapphire," and "Platinum" card market.

The Purple Card

In Brazil, Nubank's Purple Card has been a tremendous success, becoming the third most popular card and capturing 12% of the market by 2023.[180]

Initially, the team was uncertain about what features to include in the app and how much control they should give consumers over managing their own cards. On one hand, too many options could make management more complicated. The challenge was understanding what consumers actually wanted, rather than what the programmers thought they needed.

Over time, credit cards have introduced various incentives to encourage consumer spending, such as points and rewards, interest-free months, and minimum payment options. When it came to points, the recurring question was: *What do customers actually do with them?* Nubank's initial solution was radically simple: *zero fees and zero points*. They offered a straightforward product designed for the everyday consumer, fully digital, requiring only a smartphone.

---

[180] Rankings Latam. May 2024. "Credit Card Market in Brazil - 2023.12 Rankings" https://rankingslatam.com/en-mx/blogs/industry-news/credit-card-market-in-brazil-2023-12-rankings

This approach allowed Nubank to eliminate the complexity and hidden traps typically associated with traditional credit cards. By prioritizing transparency and simplicity, Nubank not only made access to credit easier but also created a clearer, fairer user experience. Without fees or confusing points programs, customers could manage their credit effectively, without any unpleasant surprises.

The Influence of Capital One

Starting a financial institution with credit cards is challenging because you cannot approve all applicants. *If you do it wrong, you could be dead in weeks*, David commented. Lending money is easy; the problem has always been getting it back.

In the evolution of credit cards, one area that has become increasingly sophisticated is the credit risk control system. This system, essential for financial institutions, is built on policies, models, and loan monitoring to assess a bank's exposure to risk.

If the risk control system is too strict, not enough cards will be issued, leading to dissatisfaction among consumers who wonder, *Why do they not accept me?* On the other hand, if the system is too lenient, the company's financial stability is endangered, with the potential for significant losses or even bankruptcy.

Today, Nubank appears to have found the right balance with its credit risk control system. By utilizing advanced technologies and innovative data analysis models, Nubank has developed a system that accurately assesses applicants' ability to repay. This approach allows the bank to offer credit cards to a larger number of people, including those with challenging credit histories, without compromising its financial security.

The Minimum Viable Product (MVP) developed was a smartphone-based digital application linked to a technological platform that enabled the issuance of a credit card, provided certain conditions were met. Initially, the team relied on credit risk models from Brazil's credit bureau system companies,[181] such as SAS, FICO, and Moody's Analytics. Although these models were the industry standard, they did not align with Nubank's objectives.

The founding team established a key principle: it was essential to respect the credit analysis models, regardless of their origin, but they had to be continuously reviewed and improved. David understood the risks of issuing credit without retail banking experience. His cautious approach led him to closely study the history of Capital One, which emerged when Signet Bank,[182] a regional bank in Richmond, Virginia, decided to spin off its credit card division as an independent subsidiary. Founded in 1994 by Richard Fairbank and Nigel Morris, Capital One became a trailblazer in data-driven innovation.

From the outset, Capital One distinguished itself by leveraging data analysis and targeted marketing. The company used risk models and customer data to segment its audience and offer tailored financial products, which allowed it to quickly expand in the credit card market. By building detailed customer

---

[181] Brazil has three large credit bureau institutions, all private, including Serasa (owned by Experian), Credit Protection Service (SPC, operated by a national association of traders) and Boa Vista SCPC, with Equifax one of the main shareholders.

[182] About Signet Bank. https://signetbank.com/en/

profiles, Capital One was able to apply highly accurate analytical models.

Eager to learn from Capital One's experience, David reached out to Nigel Morris to persuade him to invest in Nubank and assist in hiring specialized talent for credit risk management. Morris was intrigued by the idea, decided to invest, and contributed his expertise by helping recruit former Capital One employees, known for being the best in developing Credit Underwriting systems.

Credit Underwriting[183] is a critical process that involves evaluating a borrower's creditworthiness and risk before approving a loan or line of credit. This detailed assessment examines the applicant's financial and personal information to determine their risk level. Following Morris's recommendations, David consulted with top credit risk experts and brought the best specialist from Virginia to São Paulo. Together, they designed a

---

[183] Basically, a credit risk analysis process consists of:
1. Evaluation of the applicant's credit history using credit reports from credit agencies (for example, Bureau of Credit, Círculo de Crédito, or in the United States, Experian, Equifax, TransUnion). Including checking the timeliness of previous payments, existing credit levels and credit utilization.
2. Assessment of Paying Capacity. If it is possible, analyze the applicant's current income, their employment stability and other income sources, if they exist.
This leads to creating an index called Deuda-Income Ratio Evaluación (DTI) to determine the applicant's ability to handle additional payments.
3. Verification of Assets and Liabilities. Review of the applicant's assets (such as properties, investments and bonds) that can serve as a guarantee or support for the loan. And the evaluation of existing obligations and liabilities of the applicant.
4. Analysis of the general solvency of the applicant, including income stability and financial consistency. Review of any history of financial failures or defaults.

comprehensive assessment system that enabled Nubank to efficiently grant credit, ensuring safe and sustainable growth.

David had a specific request: he wanted the growth in credit issuance to be slow and steady, ensuring Nubank's survival during the critical early months. This approach led them to develop a disciplined system that, according to David, became the best credit methodology in the world.

With this system, Nubank could confidently issue credit cards while avoiding costly mistakes. The methodology, continuously refined with new data and algorithms, allowed Nubank to build a solid and loyal customer base, helping to solidify the brand.

Nubank not only revolutionized the credit card market in Brazil but also set a new industry standard in credit underwriting, proving that innovation and prudence can coexist to drive success. Most importantly, they showed that in credit risk systems, the rules were not yet set in stone.

Nubank's subscription model was also highly dynamic. As more data on transactions and customer behavior was collected, cardholders could automatically become eligible for credit limit increases. Credit limits could start as low as $14, with some gradually increasing to over $10,000, although in 2018 the average credit limit granted was $720.

> *We even tried offering credit cards with limits as low as $10, which proved quite practical and allowed these customers to gradually build their credit history,* noted David.

> *By automating this process, we solved an important problem. Brazilians were frustrated because the big banks took forever to increase their credit lines.*

In the Nubank app, cardholders can monitor in real-time how close they are to reaching their credit limit. If they were concerned about their spending, they even had the option to reduce their own credit limit.

Vitor Olivier[184], Chief Technology Officer, and one of NU's first employees, explained:

> *...we have developed tools that allow us to quickly access data. We have created a culture of decision-making based on cohort analysis—grouping customers in similar situations—which gives us data structures that remain consistent over time. As we expand our portfolio, we can run algorithms on various cohorts and test outcomes.*
>
> *This allows us to evaluate the first, second, and third-order effects of our decisions while also tracking the net present value of our customers. It is a rigorous approach to decision-making. Traditional banks have the advantage of decades of data, but our modern data infrastructure gives us the agility to experiment in ways they cannot.*

---

[184] Cfr. Chu, Michael, et al. Harvard Business School. Caso 9-321-068. Rev. Ago 2023. "Nubank: Democratizing Financial Services"

Nubank Products

Innovation is undeniably part of Nubank's DNA, driving them to continually focus on creating new products and services that improve their customers' lives. This dedication has not gone unnoticed, particularly regarding their security innovations. These features have positioned Nubank at the forefront of the industry in Latin America, as noted by Fast Company.[185] The publication ranked Nubank 22nd on its global list, highlighting features like *Modo Rua* and *Me Roubaram* (They Stole From Me).

Since the launch of its credit card, Nubank's goal has been to offer a wider range of products to its vast customer base. This diversification is crucial because the company cannot rely solely on revenue from credit card transactions. While transaction volume is undoubtedly important, it is not enough on its own.

In the financial world, there are countless products to offer, and Nubank has been steadily adding them to its portfolio. The encouraging news is that nearly all financial products have room for improvement, given that poor service is the common denominator. This creates opportunities to attract consumers by offering better experiences. The same excellent service Nubank has established with its credit card positions them well for success with their new offerings.

Although the products they have introduced currently hold a modest market share, their growth potential is significant.

---

[185] Fast Company. Mar 2024. "The most innovative companies in Latin America for 2024". https://www.fastcompany.com/91039324/latin-america-most-innovative-companies-2024

Over time, this diversification is expected to bolster their revenue streams. (See Annex 2)

At this moment, Nubank offers the following products, most of which are available only in Brazil:

1. Digital Account, which is a bank account.
2. Debit Card to access their balances.
3. Credit Card.
4. Personal Loans.
5. Savings Account.
6. Nubank Ultravioleta, a premium credit card.
7. Benefit programs with points, cashback.
8. PJ Account (Legal Entities). Bank account for small and medium-sized businesses.
9. PJ Credit Card (Legal Entities).
10. Nubank Vida: Auto and Home Insurance.
11. Nucoin Digital Currency, Cryptocurrencies.
12. Investments: ETF management.
13. Build Limit Function: Loans secured with collateral.

The Ultravioleta

In July 2021, Nubank launched its Ultravioleta card in Brazil, featuring the sleek black version of the MasterCard logo[186]. The idea was to democratize access to the Black card[187]

---

[186] MasterCard has two logos for its cards, one with the familiar orange and yellow circles and a similar one, but in shades of silver color, which are for premium level cards, called Black.

[187] "Black service" generally refers to a category of premium services offered by financial institutions, generally banks, to their high-net-worth customers. These services are designed to offer a more exclusive and personalized experience, with additional benefits that are not available to the standard customer.

PRODUCT INNOVATION

for its customers—an option typically reserved for those who meet the high requirements of traditional banks was now available to a broader audience.

The Ultravioleta card was considered high-end, crafted from metal and boasting a refined design, with several notable benefits. One of its standout features was its cashback,[188] which, unlike most cards, automatically converted into an investment with a 200% return on the CDI (Brazil's Interbank Deposit Certificate).[189]

Cristina remarked on the cashback:

> *My cashback is never coming out of there; that money is out of sight! Because, where else are you going to find a return like that? Nowhere.*

It is undoubtedly a very good gain. In a market where finding a return of 120% or 130% of the CDI is already notable, reaching 200% seems utopian.

Indeed, it offers an exceptional return. In a market where returns of 120% or 130% of the CDI are already impressive, achieving 200% seems almost utopian.

---

[188] Cashback on a credit card refers to a benefit from which the holder receives a percentage of the money spent on purchases as a refund. This percentage varies depending on the type of card and the type of purchase. For example, some cards offer a higher percentage of cashback in specific categories such as supermarkets, gasoline or restaurants.

[189] CDI refers to 'Interbank Deposit Certificates.' CDIs are financial instruments used between banking institutions for short-term loans. They are considered a key reference point for the interest rate in the Brazilian financial market. As of June 2024, it stood at 10.40% annually.

However, Nubank understood that to attract and retain these high-profile clients, it needed more than just an attractive card and appealing cashback. The Ultravioleta, with all its premium features, was only the beginning. The real strategy was to build strong, lasting relationships with these customers, offering them not just financial perks, but an unparalleled customer experience.

At the same time, the Ultravioleta card represents Nubank's commitment to being a comprehensive financial institution, catering to all markets and all people.

Here are some of the card's key features:[190]

- **Material**: The NU Ultravioleta card is made from stainless steel, with a darker violet hue compared to the traditional purple card, giving it a more premium, durable appearance and feel than standard plastic cards.
- **Rewards Benefits**: The card offers an attractive rewards program, including 1% cashback on all purchases. This cashback earns interest at 200% of the CDI on business days and never expires.
- **Insurance and Protection**: It comes with travel insurance and purchase protection, covering everything from trip cancellations to theft or damage of items bought with the card.
- **VIP Lounge Access**: Ultravioleta cardholders often enjoy access to VIP lounges at airports, adding an extra layer of comfort and convenience while traveling.

---

[190] Nubank. Ultravioleta. Abr 2024. https://blog.nubank.com.br/cartao-nubank-ultravioleta-tudo-sobre/

- **Personalized Attention**: Users of the Ultravioleta card receive more personalized, priority customer service.
- **Higher Credit Limits**: The card generally offers higher credit limits than standard cards, providing greater spending flexibility.

Checking and Savings Account

The checking and savings account posed a significant challenge for Nubank, as we have previously mentioned, primarily due to the need to secure a banking license. However, once Nubank obtained the license, they quickly launched their checking and savings account, known as NU Conta.

Unlike the inherent complexity of credit cards, the checking and savings account was designed with efficient simplicity in mind. It aimed to welcome anyone who wanted to open an account, offering not only a safe place to store money and make payments but also providing one of the best savings and investment instruments accessible to all. As customer relationships deepened, Nubank could then offer additional services, such as credit cards, thereby reducing the risk factor. In Nubank's case, however, this process was reversed: they first offered credit cards, and, thanks to the trust they built, customers were more inclined to open a checking or savings account.

In October 2017, Nubank launched its second product: a digital checking and savings account that was easy to open but came with two key features. First, balances earned interest based on the overnight interbank loan rates of the Brazilian banking system, which were 9.93% in 2017 and 6.42% in 2018. By 2024, these rates had risen to 11% annually. Secondly, there were no transaction fees, except for cash withdrawals at ATMs, where Nubank passed on the fee charged by the ATM's bank (approximately $1.78). All other services—such as utility bill payments, transfers to merchants, friends, and family, as well as deposits—were free of charge. Additionally, the digital account offered access to a debit card for convenient transactions.

Nubank's approach stood in stark contrast to traditional banking practices. Conventional banks typically offered checking accounts with little to no interest, often attaching symbolic rates for those maintaining minimum balances. They also charged monthly management fees that could easily consume any returns.

Our initial motivation for offering a savings product was to support our credit card business through customer deposits while providing a fair return on their savings, along with daily liquidity, explained Vitor Olivier, who by August 2018 had become the general manager of Nubank's digital account product.

Simplicity was key to Nubank's success. Traditional banks overwhelmed customers with acronyms and excessive information, making financial services feel inaccessible. Nubank's straightforward strategy fostered financial inclusion and attracted customers who had yet to adopt its signature purple credit cards. *In a couple of months, we gained over a million customers by listening to their needs and adapting to them*, Olivier said.

By the end of 2018, deposits in Nubank accounts totaled $628.8 million. By March 2024, those deposits had skyrocketed to $24.3 billion.[191] *We also noticed that each group of customers*

---

[191] NU Q1 2024 Earnings Presentation.

gradually increased their average balances and transaction rates, engaging more in activities like debit purchases, fund transfers, and bill payments. In fact, newer customer groups started with higher balances than those who came before them, Olivier added.

In this way, Nubank not only developed an accessible and beneficial financial product but also built a lasting relationship of trust and steady growth with its customers.

Foreign Exchange Market

NuInvest, Nubank's investment brokerage,[192] recently received authorization from the Central Bank of Brazil to operate in the foreign exchange market.[193] This approval, published on Friday, April 19, 2024, in the Official Gazette of the Union,[194] represents a significant milestone in Nubank's continued operational expansion.

---

[192] An investment broker, also known as a stockbroker or securities broker, is a financial professional who acts as an intermediary between buyers and sellers of securities, such as stocks, bonds, mutual funds, and other financial instruments. Their primary function is to facilitate transactions in the securities market and provide financial advice to their clients.

[193] The foreign exchange market, also known as Forex (short for Foreign Exchange), is a global decentralized market where the currencies of different countries are traded. It is the largest and most liquid financial market in the world, with a daily transaction volume exceeding 6 trillion dollars.

[194] Latam Fintech. Apr. 2024. "NuInvest, Nubank's investment broker, received authorization from the Central Bank to operate in the foreign exchange market in Brazil." https://www.latamfintech.co/articles/nuinvest-el-broker-de-inversiones-de-nubank-recibio-la-autorizacion-del-banco-central-para-operar-en-el-mercado-de-divisas-en-brasil

Nubank acquired the investment broker Easynvest in September 2020, with the transaction finalizing in June 2021. Following the acquisition, the brokerage was rebranded as NuInvest. Easynvest had previously served 150,000 active clients, but by 2024, Nubank had grown that base to an impressive 15 million active clients—highlighting the direct impact of Nubank's broad customer reach and growing interest in financial products.

As part of its global strategy, Nubank integrated NuInvest[195] directly into its main application, centralizing its investment services and making them easily accessible to all of its clients in Brazil.

Brazil's foreign exchange market is expansive, with 175 entities authorized to operate, according to data from the Central Bank. These include banks, exchange agents, brokers, dealers (DTVM),[196] financial institutions, and development agencies.

In the realm of cryptocurrencies, Nubank has also made significant strides. More than two million people in Brazil have purchased cryptocurrencies through Nubank's platform, which currently focuses on Bitcoin and Ethereum. Demand for these

---

[195] Easynvest was one of the first companies to offer online access to the stock market in 1999 and the first to offer mobile access to the fixed income market in 2016. It held a leadership position in the development of technology and innovations in financial services in Brazil. On the Easynvest platform, clients could evaluate, compare, and invest in a wide range of financial instruments, including public securities, private securities, and mutual funds, as well as trade stocks, options, and futures.
[196] In Brazil, DTVM refers to "Distribuidora de Títulos e Valores Mobiliários." These institutions are authorized by the Central Bank of Brazil to operate in the financial and capital markets. Their primary function is to intermediate the purchase and sale of securities and financial instruments, such as stocks, bonds, and other financial instruments. DTVMs can also offer portfolio management and financial advisory services.

assets has been substantial, with more Brazilians investing in cryptocurrencies than in the stock market—a trend that Nubank has successfully capitalized on.

The market response was swift: within a month, over a million customers were buying cryptocurrencies through Nubank. NU's strategy in the crypto space avoids oversaturating the market with low-value coins or "memecoins,"[197] choosing instead to focus on resilient assets with established trading volumes. This approach reflects Nubank's concern for its customers, recognizing that the average Brazilian investor has limited knowledge of cryptocurrencies. NU aims to offer a safer and more reliable approach to these digital assets.

New Services

In one of his most candid interviews, David revealed that being seen as outsiders in the financial industry profoundly shaped Nubank's culture and decision-making in its early years. According to David, repeatedly hearing from industry veterans that their venture was impossible made him hesitant to work with people who had experience in the field. As a result, the initial team, during the first two or three years, was made up entirely of outsiders, driven by the belief that they needed to reinvent everything from the ground up.

---

[197] A memecoin is a type of cryptocurrency created from an internet meme or joke, and not necessarily for its underlying technology or use case. Memecoins gain popularity mainly due to their viral appeal, often through the support of online communities and influential figures. An iconic example is Dogecoin, which was inspired by the Shiba Inu dog meme.

A clear example of this was when they built their collection system literally from scratch. The process was incredibly challenging, as they had no prior knowledge of how to do it. It ended up taking them three years to complete. David acknowledged that this was a costly lesson. What an industry expert could have explained in fifteen minutes, they had to figure out through painstaking trial and error.[198]

It was too extreme, David admitted. *You don't need to reinvent everything; you just need to innovate in the key areas where you truly want to break barriers. I wish we had started with a better balance of internal and external people.* Over time, he realized that the imbalance between the ability to question and the experience to provide answers was a critical lesson learned.

Nubank Shopping

The next innovative service introduced by Nubank was Nubank Shopping, a digital shopping mall within the Nubank app, accessible through a shopping bag icon at the bottom of the screen. Currently, this feature is only available in Brazil.[199]

The concept is simple yet effective: a virtual mall offering a wide range of products, in partnership with various stores, providing customers with secure shopping, competitive prices, and better control over their expenses. With more than 180 stores, Nubank Shopping also offers special discounts and even cashback, which is credited directly within the app.[200]

---

[198] Cfr. Entrevista a David. Fintech Nexus. Jun 2022. How this Digital Bank Brought Millions of People into the Financial System, Nubank. https://www.youtube.com/watch?v=yXLWiqPEt6U
[199] Nubank. Nu Shopping. https://nubank.com.br/nu-shopping/
[200] Cfr. Nubank. Nu Shopping.

PRODUCT INNOVATION

Although Nubank does not handle delivery logistics or product warranties, it serves as an ideal platform for businesses to reach millions of customers without requiring significant marketing investments.

Launched in November 2022, Nubank Shopping features several product categories such as fashion, gaming, travel, and pet care. Customers can shop easily and securely while benefiting from discounts, coupons, and rebates.

In just one year since its launch, Nubank Shopping reached a historic milestone with 255 million visits in 2023.[201]

To enhance its offerings and better meet customer needs, NU collects detailed data, including the top-selling products from the last 90 days. These include appliances, smartphones, kitchen utensils, smart TVs, and beauty and personal care products. Additionally, they observed a surge in searches for tech products like TVs, air conditioners, and laptops, reflecting key consumer trends in Brazil.

With its large customer base, vast data pool, and powerful data analysis system, Nubank appears to have all the necessary elements for continued business success.

---

[201] Nubank. Nubank Shopping. Mar 2024. https://international.nubank.com.br/consumers/nubank-shopping-reaches-255-million-visits-in-2023/

Digital Personal Banker

One of the projects that excites David the most is the idea of an artificial intelligence robot providing expert financial advice to Nubank's clients. *Imagine this: Nubank customers, who have already taken the important step of getting a card, will now have a technological ally focused on financial inclusion.* [202]

Globally, the lack of financial education is a pressing issue. While providing access to the financial system is a significant achievement, teaching people how to use it efficiently and manage their money wisely is another challenge altogether.

Many people face complex financial questions, such as:

– *Who offers me the best loan?*
– *How do I organize my finances to improve my financial health?*
– *How can I manage my money to reduce my tax burden?*

These are the kinds of questions that only expert financial advisors typically answer, and until now, this exclusive advice has been available only to the wealthiest 1% through private banking.

This is where Nubank's revolutionary proposal comes in: artificial intelligence functioning as a private banker, accessible to every client right from their smartphone. Mobile phones have already made it possible for everyone to carry a bank branch in

---

[202] De la C, Juan Carlos. Entrevista con David. Imagen Radio. May 2024. "Crecimiento de Nubank en México, Colombia y Brasil.
https://youtu.be/wPUBO20vxJk?si=rwcEEy92HtYYtDvx

their pocket. So why not also have a personal banker? That is the next step.

It is a bold and complex idea, but technological advancements are making this digital financial advisor more achievable. To create something like this, you would need market data, customer financial data, and generative artificial intelligence capable of analyzing the information and providing coherent responses. These are the essential components to bring this AI Banker to life—and NU already possesses all of them.

The future where every Nubank customer can access direct, personalized financial advice, regardless of their income level, is closer than we think. With this initiative, Nubank aims not only to bring more people into the financial system but also to empower them with the knowledge they need to make smarter financial decisions.[203]

Consumer Protection

Edward Wible played a pivotal role in developing innovative features for Nubank's products. One of his most significant contributions was integrating artificial intelligence technology to automate credit analysis, allowing Nubank to deliver fast and accurate decisions to its customers.

Scalability and Security

---

[203] Cfr. De la C, Juan Carlos. Entrevista con David. Imagen Radio. May 2024

In addition to developing the application, the goal was to undertake careful planning across several critical areas. First and foremost, the aim was to build an application capable of scaling to handle millions of users without crashing, which required an extremely robust and flexible technological architecture. This included implementing load balancing solutions, distributed databases, and a cloud infrastructure that could dynamically adjust to fluctuating traffic demands.

Equally important was the emphasis on security. Every component of the application needed to adhere to an advanced security strategy designed to protect sensitive data from potential breaches. This involved encrypting data both in transit and at rest, implementing multi-factor authentication, and conducting regular security audits to identify and address vulnerabilities.

The planning process focused not only on ensuring the application's scalability and ability to accommodate a large user base but also on maintaining the highest levels of security and resilience, thus guaranteeing the service's integrity and availability at all times.

Modo Rua

In 2022, Brazil experienced a surge in mobile phone thefts, with incidents occurring approximately every three minutes. As more people linked their financial information to their phones, Nubank recognized the urgency of addressing this issue in its largest and fastest-growing market. This sparked a year of innovative and practical security solutions, driven by customer feedback in Brazil, Mexico, and Colombia.[204]

The first of these innovations was *Modo Rua*, launched in January 2023 ahead of Carnival, a time notorious for increased theft. This feature was developed in response to customers who, for safety reasons, would log out of or delete the app before leaving home. *Modo Rua* offered a more convenient solution by allowing users to set limits on payment amounts and the number of transactions when not connected to a trusted Wi-Fi network. The feature was quickly embraced, with 300,000 users during Carnival and more than a million by the end of 2023.

To implement new services, we hold ourselves to a very high standard, constantly asking: Does this feature truly meet a need? David remarked in an interview. *Modo Rua* was something entirely new to the market, and now four other banks have adopted a similar feature. Its popularity allowed Nubank to continue introducing new functionalities, such as marking safe locations and hiding balances within the app.

Me Roubaram

Nubank also introduced the *Me Roubaram* (They Stole from Me) feature, accessible through a specially enabled webpage, where customers could quickly report and deactivate a lost or stolen card.

---

[204] Salazar, David. FastCompany. "How Nubank is making digital transactions safer for cellphone users", Mar 2024.
https://www.fastcompany.com/91040515/nubank-most-innovative-companies-2024

They later launched temporary Virtual Credit Cards that expire after 24 hours, offering additional protection by safeguarding real card numbers during online transactions. Another innovation was the *Alô Protegido* (Hello Protected) feature, which helps prevent phone scams by screening incoming calls and blocking potential fraud attempts.

Nubank's goal with these security features is to seamlessly integrate them into customers' daily lives. *How well-equipped is a Nubank consumer to manage their security in this digital world?* David posed. Identifying needs and developing innovative solutions has been central to the company's continued growth.

Financial Inclusion

David once recalled something Cristina had told him:

The pain of customers is the same, regardless of the country. (...) There is a lot of pain in Latin America. It is probably the best market in the world for our business because we can free millions of unbanked people from their difficult situations, marked by high-interest rates and poor customer service.

This great challenge, which forms the foundation of Nubank's mission, also highlighted a deeper issue: the vast population excluded from the financial system. Nubank's initial goal was to help those already within the banking system who were mistreated by excessive fees and subpar service from traditional banks. However, they also recognized the significant number of people outside the system—individuals who are rarely served by banks or the government. While this problem is widely acknowledged, little action is taken to address it because doing so is often seen as unprofitable and costly for both governments and traditional banks. Despite various initiatives in many developing countries, progress remains limited.

For Nubank, this challenge also presented a compelling business opportunity. They discovered that many individuals had once been part of the banking system but were expelled due to negative credit histories. Traditional banks do little to bring these people back, as they are often "marked." In the best-case scenario, there is a chance for them to re-enter the system when credit bureaus activate the "forget clause" or credit clearing, which erases records with no activity after seven or more years of default. This allows these individuals to attempt a fresh start. However, this opportunity is rare—many are unaware of this lifeline, and even when their credit history is cleared, banks tend to view those with a "blank credit history" as risky, especially if their age or other factors suggest they are not newcomers to the system. As a result, they are seldom granted credit again.

Nubank, however, found a way to offer these individuals a second chance through a new credit analysis model. One method is through a secured credit product called the "Build Limit Function," where the client deposits a certain amount as collateral. Over time, as they manage their account responsibly, they gradually regain credibility within the system. Another approach is offering low credit limits, allowing these individuals to rebuild their credit over time and regain their status as full participants in the financial system.

Similarly, Nubank also focused on another key group: young adults who have just come of age or are entering the job market for the first time, and therefore have no credit history. Nubank provides them with the opportunity to start building their credit from scratch.

A third group includes older adults who have never had a credit card—whether due to working in the informal economy or other reasons—who now wish to obtain one, drawn by the advantages Nubank offers. This group also includes those living in areas with limited or no access to traditional bank branches.

This was made possible by the sophistication of Nubank's credit analysis model, which, unlike traditional models, incorporates a wide range of variables. This approach allows for a more accurate assessment of each individual's unique circumstances, offering a truer reflection of their financial situation.

As a result of this strategy, Nubank was able to bring 5.7 million people into the financial system within just one year, providing them with first-class credit card services that come without abusive interest rates or hidden fees. Remarkably, they achieved this without incurring additional costs, relying on government programs, or sacrificing profitability—proving that financial inclusion can be both impactful and commercially viable.

In Mexico in 2017, only 36.9% of the population had a bank account, leaving over 63% of the population unbanked—making it the worst performer in Latin America in terms of financial inclusion. Fortunately, this has been changing. By 2021, the Financial Inclusion Survey[205] showed that 49.1% of the population had access to some form of financial product, reducing the unbanked population to 50.9% among those aged 18 to 70.

For Nubank, financial inclusion is an important goal.

As we have discussed, financial inclusion remains a significant global challenge. Jay Rosengard,[206] Director of the Financial Sector Program at the Harvard Kennedy School, emphasized during a conference at Sibos Spotlight:

Financial inclusion means ensuring access to formal financial services for everyone, especially low-income households and small businesses. This is critical because in many countries, these groups represent the majority of the population and economic activity.

Rosengard explained that the most essential financial services include payment services (such as money transfers, bill payments, and remittances); savings accounts (for emergencies, retirement, and specific expenses); and microcredit. Equally important are services that mitigate risk, like auto, life, and health insurance.

---

[205] INEGI. 2021. Encuesta nacional de inclusión financiera (enif), 2021 principales resultados.
https://www.inegi.org.mx/contenidos/saladeprensa/boletines/2022/enif/ENIF 21.pdf

[206] Rosengard, Jay. SibosTV. Conference Sibos Spotlight. Oct 2014. "What is financial inclusion and why should we care?".
https://www.youtube.com/watch?v=BGNDQtHyasw

The true innovation, he noted, lies in tailoring these services to the conditions and preferences of low-income markets—designing products and delivery systems that are financially sustainable. Sustainability is vital because long-term reliance on external support is often not feasible.

For Nubank, however, these initiatives are entirely viable. The company has successfully integrated millions of people into the financial system who previously lacked access to financial products. By 2024, Nubank had brought 21.5 million customers into the financial fold, many of whom had never before held a financial product.

NU Technology

Nubank started with no technology whatsoever. That was Edward's task: to sit down and create a technological plan while simultaneously developing the first product, the credit card.

The first major decision was to leverage cloud technology. They opted to build their infrastructure on distributed computing using Amazon Web Services (AWS), which allowed for rapid scalability and greater flexibility.

From the outset, Edward prioritized security while ensuring a seamless and transparent user experience.

Edward's vision for Nubank was to create a financial institution that fully embraced its financial responsibility and regulatory compliance in a completely integrated manner. This was no small feat, but starting from scratch gave them the perfect opportunity to build these principles into all their processes from the very beginning.

This plan included conducting their own "Know Your Customer" (KYC) processes,[207] combating money laundering, working directly with regulators, and producing regulatory

---

[207] KYC, or "Know Your Customer," is a process used by financial institutions and other entities to verify the identity of their clients. This process is crucial for preventing fraud, money laundering, terrorist financing, and other financial crimes. It is mandatory and falls under anti-money laundering (AML) laws and anti-terrorist financing regulations. Through KYC, companies collect and verify personal information from clients, such as identification documents, proof of address, and financial details.

reports. Their goal was to maintain a first-class record-keeping system, ensuring full control over the financial relationship with their customers. This approach allowed them to retain complete oversight of their financial operations while prioritizing customer security.

In an interview, Edward remarked:

> *There is a strong trend among many fintechs to avoid being classified as banks. Their reasons may be legitimate—they want to sidestep Basel regulations[208] capital requirements, and other costly regulations. While these arguments are understandable, Nubank believed that complying with and controlling all these regulatory and financial prudence elements was essential for maintaining a solid business model. Recent examples have shown that models failing to control these aspects, such as service providers or market makers involved in peer-to-peer lending, tend to be fragile.*[209]

---

[208] The headquarters of the Basel Committee on Banking Supervision is located in the city of Basel, Switzerland. This is why the set of recommendations issued by this Committee is called Basel. These recommendations are intended to strengthen the regulation, supervision, and risk management of the banking sector worldwide. Known as Basel I, II, and III, these guidelines aim to ensure financial stability by implementing minimum capital requirements, proper management of credit, operational, and market risks, and improvements in financial transparency and disclosure. Their main goal is to increase the resilience of banks to potential financial crises, promoting a safer and more robust banking system.

[209] SE Daily. Software Engineering Daily. Jul 2018. Podcast. "Build a Bank: Nubank with Edward Wible".
https://softwareengineeringdaily.com/2018/07/10/build-a-bank-nubank-with-edward-wible/

NU's goal is to be both a true financial institution and a technology company that functions as a financial institution. This combination allows them to offer high-quality financial services while ensuring security and stability in their operations.

From the outset, Edward had a clear vision for the product they needed to create: a credit card. However, he recalled:

> We simply didn't know how to build it, nor did we know how to scale it. Learning the model and mastering it was probably the hardest part. We started with a microservices architecture but made mistakes with the context boundaries in various ways.
>
> (...)
>
> One particular challenge was modeling the concept of money. "Initially, we thought of it as an integer with cents," Edward explained, "but then we discovered there are fractional cents, like those used in Facebook ads. That was a hassle. I still remember the moment the team realized we had made that mistake.[210]

Another hurdle was properly sizing some services—something that seemed trivial but turned out to be a significant headache. These challenges highlighted the need for *decades of financial experience* to build such programs. It wasn't easy because the team lacked that experience; it was a real challenge.

Initially, they created a service called "accounts" to handle all the accounts within the system. However, they soon realized this service needed to be broken down into many

---

[210] Cfr. SE Daily. Software Engineering Daily. Jul 2018

separate "accounts." It wasn't just one service—they needed specific accounts for everything, including billing, order lines, and credit cards. Each had its own unique structure and couldn't be grouped together. While their original intention was to build a solution based on microservices architecture, they ended up with an *accidental monolith*.[211]

This problem is common in startups when they launch an application with a simple architecture to quickly enter the market. Initially, this architecture is sufficient. However, as the application gains users and new features are added, the codebase expands in an unstructured manner. Instead of breaking the application into smaller, manageable services (as in a microservices architecture), all functionalities are added to a single codebase. Over time, this leads to an *accidental monolith*, which becomes increasingly difficult to manage or maintain.

Part of the challenge the team faced was the uncertainty about scale, performance requirements, and how best to decompose the components.

Another critical aspect of entering the market quickly was building a MasterCard authorizer. This process required setting up a physical data center, securing at least one communication line, and importing specialized hardware from the United States. Simply getting the hardware through Brazilian customs could have taken months, potentially ruining their carefully planned schedule

---

[211] In the context of systems and software development, an "accidental monolith" refers to an application that, due to rapid growth and unplanned design decisions, becomes a monolithic structure. This results in a system with strong coupling, meaning that the components are strongly dependent on one another, which is why it is difficult to scale and maintain, due to the lack of modularity and adequate refactoring during its expansion.

To avoid these delays, they decided to integrate their system with a third party that already had an operational authorizer. Although this decision felt like making a deal with the devil, it ultimately saved the company. They do not regret the choice, even though it led to challenges with scaling and managing the transition, as they were dependent on a third party for the registry system, which controlled and backed the data. The transition became incredibly difficult and only became viable after they implemented their own authorizer infrastructure two years later.

Despite encountering obstacles in nearly every process, through trial and error, the engineering team learned, analyzed, and adapted. This experience ultimately made them extremely efficient, resulting in first-class technology.

Security at NU

Nubank, like all financial companies worldwide, understands that security is an endless task. *We will never reach a point where we can say, 'Ah! We made it; that's enough,* Edward remarked with a touch of irony.

At NU, they have embraced a broader security culture, moving beyond merely reacting to incidents. They maintain a dedicated team working on security full-time. While they may be safer than most companies, they can never say this with certainty because the risks are always present.

Their adversaries are constantly evolving, growing in capability and sophistication. To stay ahead, Nubank applies the latest technologies in pursuit of its goals. *It's like a game of cops and robbers, an endless game*, Edward noted. The stakes are high, especially in banking, where the business revolves around money, making it a prime target for thieves. That's why NU takes security extremely seriously.

Nubank benefits from key advantages due to its modern technology. They built everything from scratch, avoiding the pitfalls of old systems or outsourced solutions. Every component was handcrafted by their team, meticulously assembled bit by bit, allowing them to have a deep understanding of every part of their systems. Unlike many financial institutions that acquire applications or rely on market solutions, Nubank knows its systems inside and out.

Security issues often arise in institutions with numerous interconnected systems and subsystems, especially when these systems expose a broad surface of various applications. In many financial institutions, legacy systems and continuous updates unintentionally create critical vulnerabilities that aren't fully understood. This complexity often requires specialists with specific knowledge of each system or application. When these specialists leave the company, they leave behind knowledge gaps, or worse, only one person understands the system, and they cannot retire because no one else knows how to fix it.

At Nubank, they have worked hard to foster a culture that avoids these pitfalls as much as possible. They ensure that multiple people understand how everything works, avoiding reliance on a single engineer for each area. Moreover, their architecture is more homogeneous—each service is similar to the others, meaning that solving a security issue in one area often solves it across the system.

It seems the key to security lies in leveraging new technology, consistently applying patches and updates, and maintaining a homogeneous architecture. Nubank also emphasizes the importance of getting encryption right and avoiding mistakes. For instance, they use Mutual TLS[212] — a powerful technology that enhances network communication security by requiring mutual authentication of all parties involved—along with other advanced technologies. However, what matters most is their ability to continuously evolve and advance rapidly, ensuring top-tier security for their customers.

Recently, Nubank introduced a geolocation feature within the app to help reduce fraud. By knowing a customer's location, the app can assess whether a purchase on their statement was truly made by them. While this feature provides an added layer of security, it has sparked some privacy concerns.[213]

When NU defines the nature of their business, they say:

...more than a bank, we are a technology company that just happens to be in the financial sector.

Indeed, NU is a high-tech company functioning as a bank, with each customer's smartphone serving as their branch. Everything revolves around their app, which is central to their strategy.

---

[212] Mutual TLS (Transport Layer Security), also known as mutual authentication or client certificate authentication, is a way to secure communications over a network by authenticating both the client and the server during the establishment of the TLS connection. Unlike standard TLS, where only the server authenticates to the client, in Mutual TLS both ends of the communication verify each other.

[213] Cfr. The Brief. "O que o CTO da Nubank pensa sobre atendimento ao cliente"

The NU app is the heart of the customer experience. It is simple, intuitive, and comprehensive —designed to meet all the needs of their clients. Yet, crafting this simplicity has been an art in itself, as they strive to avoid overwhelming users by presenting everything in one place, carefully balancing ease of use with functionality.

Nubank's technological success can be largely attributed to Edward Wible, the company's first software engineer and inaugural CIO (Chief Information Officer). Edward was the architect behind Nubank's technological infrastructure and helped shape its engineering culture during the early days of this disruptive fintech.

Although Edward is no longer responsible for CIO duties, he continues to play a critical role as Chief Engineering Officer. Since 2020, the position of CIO has been held by Jagpreet Duggal. A mechanical engineer who graduated from Yale University, Duggal ensures that Nubank's technological infrastructure meets the day-to-day needs of the business. His responsibilities include overseeing IT operations and information management, while collaborating closely with operations, human resources, and finance to ensure that the technology supports every aspect of the company's functions.

Nubank also has a separate role for innovation and long-term technology strategy—the CTO (Chief Technology Officer). Since December 2022, this role has been held by Vitor Olivier, who focuses on driving the company's future technological direction.

Technological Risks

A digital bank, by its nature, depends entirely on digital services.

Over time, traditional banks have become more technical and automated, with their data and processing housed in highly secure data centers. These centers, along with their backup sites, are often located in remote, bunker-like facilities designed to minimize the risk of data loss or operational failure.

The advent of cloud computing brought a radical shift in infrastructure, replacing the traditional server and database systems with more advanced commercial cloud services. These ultramodern data centers are continuously updated with the latest hardware and software, located in secret locations, and monitored 24/7 with extensive safeguards. Built for resilience, they feature redundant power, cooling, and connectivity between centers, along with robust protection against digital attacks.

While risks exist in any facility, these cloud services offer much greater mitigation than what a single institution could manage on its own when securing IT assets. Additionally, they allow companies to implement their own, often redundant, security protocols—further enhancing protection.

Nubank relies heavily on data centers operated by AWS[214] and other external providers for Internet access and cloud

---

[214] AWS (*Amazon Web Services*) is a cloud computing services platform offered by Amazon. It provides a wide range of services, including storage, computing, databases, analysis, networks, development tools, artificial intelligence and more, which allow companies to scale and grow in a flexible and profitable way.

computing. Any disruption to these services could significantly impact its business operations.

The continuity of Nubank's transaction processing systems is critical, as its customer-facing applications depend on third-party-managed systems and facilities. Continuous Internet access and sufficient bandwidth are essential to maintain connectivity. Interruptions to these services can result in customer dissatisfaction, loss of business, and damage to its reputation. Although Nubank closely monitors its providers, it cannot fully control their security measures, potentially facing challenges in disaster recovery and system management.

Providers may experience issues such as outages, performance errors, security breaches, or natural disasters, which are difficult to detect and resolve quickly. Any disruption in these services could hinder Nubank's ability to deliver reliable solutions, increase operational costs, and harm its reputation—potentially leading customers to seek alternatives and permanently impacting its business.

Management and Operation

Nubankers

NU has cultivated a strong organizational culture, starting with a focus on internal branding that fosters a deep sense of belonging, motivation, and alignment with the company's values and goals.

> *A Nubanker is anyone who works at NU, regardless of nationality, position, or area of expertise. Everyone is equally important. Far from being mere cogs in a machine, Nubankers are individuals with autonomy and freedom, all working toward a common goal, with the ability to contribute and participate in decisions that are transforming the lives of millions of Mexicans.*[215]

As of 2024, Nubank had approximately 7,700 Nubankers, a team made up of 41% women and 59% men, representing over 30 nationalities. One of Nubank's gender equity goals is to achieve at least 50% women in leadership positions by 2025.

Culturally, NU places a high value on diversity, believing that diversity of all kinds makes them stronger, leading to better decisions and broader perspectives. For NU, diversity goes

---

[215] Nubank. Blog. Sobre la voz Nubanker. "Ya somos más de 1000 Nubankers en México" https://blog.nu.com.mx/ya-somos-mas-de-1000-nubankers-en-mexico/#

beyond gender—it encompasses thought, experience, and beliefs, fostering a meritocratic culture centered around ideas. Their long-term vision is to achieve a 50/50 gender balance.[216]

In 2016, after an $80 million funding round, David used part of the investment to hire hundreds of tech workers and opened an office in Germany to tap into additional talent.[217]

Having 7,700 employees may seem conservative for a financial institution serving over 100 million customers, but Nubank's ability to manage such a large customer base with a relatively small staff is remarkable. The company is especially praised for its excellent, 100% human-driven customer service. This success is largely due to Nubank's strong focus on automation and advanced technology, which streamlines processes.

From the start, David emphasized the importance of the composition of Nubank's staff, prioritizing quality over quantity. "We must have strong and diverse teams," he said, highlighting one of Nubank's five core values.

Nubank operates with small, specialized teams focused on specific areas, with a strong emphasis on diversity—understood as cognitive diversity,[218] which includes different ideas, professions, educational backgrounds, and specialties. This approach drives creativity and fosters innovative solutions to the

---

[216] Cfr. Blu Radio. Colombia. Jun 2023. Entrevista a David.
https://www.youtube.com/watch?v=cc1XVbb1TJ8&t=1159s
[217] Cfr. Kauflin, Jeff. Forbes. Abr 2021. "How David Built The World's Most Valuable Digital Bank And Became A Billionaire".
https://www.forbes.com/sites/jeffkauflin/2021/04/07/fintech-billionaire-david-velez-nubank-brazil-digital-bank/?sh=195970646b27
[218] Cfr. Op. Cit. Trava, Oswaldo, Podcast. Abr. 2020.

company's challenges. The variety of viewpoints ensures that different ideas are considered, ultimately leading to the best decisions, as everyone's input is valued, regardless of who had the original idea.

Nubank promotes the belief that while people should hold strong convictions and ideas, they must also be open to the possibility of being wrong. They seek individuals with compelling arguments who possess the humility and intelligence to consider other perspectives, and, if necessary, admit mistakes. Listening to and accepting different viewpoints is fundamental to their culture.

Nubank started with just 12 employees, but this small team quickly expanded due to the company's rapid growth. However, finding the right type of collaborators was no easy task.

David placed great importance on nurturing those initial hires, putting considerable effort into the process because he saw them as the foundation for the future. These early employees would set the tone for the next 20 or 30 years of Nubank's growth. Those who passed the involuntary filters—working out of the house on California Street, embracing the challenge of building a bank from scratch, or accepting that Nubank didn't resemble a traditional financial institution—were offered 20% more than their previous salaries and even company shares. This ensured a strong and lasting commitment.

The urgent mission was to instill Nubank's corporate culture within the first few months. The values of challenging the status quo and questioning conventional beliefs became embedded in the company's DNA. At Nubank, when someone says something can't be done, the response is: *Yes, we can.* This revolutionary mindset drives them not to settle but to continually strive for improvement.

This is how Nubank's first 12 employees hired the next 100, and then 200, helping to scale the company while instilling the essential culture needed for growth. The paradox was that this active, dynamic group could seem difficult to align and manage, but this challenge was carefully handled. They sought *people with minds full of questions*,[219] those with the humility to learn and the openness to understand that someone else might have the right answer. This approach ensured that, despite the diversity and energy of the team, cultural coherence and a spirit of constant innovation were maintained.

> *As organizations grow, inertia and bureaucracy tend to creep in, and things inevitably break. The instinct is often to create more processes, which in turn generate even more inertia, leading to a cycle of process creation.*
>
> *To combat this, it is crucial to be intentional in identifying where unnecessary processes have infiltrated and to eliminate them. First, it involves empowering everyone in the organization to speak up when they encounter unnecessary bureaucracy. Second, it's essential to preserve the entrepreneurial DNA within the organization. This ensures that, despite growth and expansion, the innovative and agile spirit*

---

[219] Endevor Colombia. #HighImpactGala2023. Oct 2023. "David de Nubank: Impulsando la Transformación Financiera en Latam".
https://www.youtube.com/watch?v=W7zGGhpKnu4

that has characterized Nubank since its inception is maintained.

(...) We have a Slack[220] channel called 'Bureaucracy Hunters,' where people literally come in and say, 'I don't understand why this process exists,' and we go and remove it.[221]

From the beginning, Nubank didn't seek people with all the answers but rather individuals with a beginner's mindset—similar to the Japanese Zen concept of "Shoshin" or *Beginner's Mind*,[222] —where humility, curiosity, and openness are valued, and freedom from preconceived notions is encouraged.

This approach proved invaluable not only for the company's development but also for fostering a growth-oriented mindset and a deeper appreciation for daily experiences across all areas of Nubank's corporate life. The beginner's mindset allowed employees to be treated with respect and dignity, reinforcing the company's core principles.

This ethos of humility and curiosity was key to building a strong corporate culture at Nubank, where every team member felt valued and motivated to contribute to the collective success. As a result, the company grew not only in size but also in the

---

[220] Slack is a business communication and collaboration tool, owned by Salesforce, that has become a key piece in team and project management in many organizations.
[221] Cfr. Morris, Nigel. Entrevista con David Vélez. Fintech Nexus. Jun 2022.
[222] The concept of *"Beginners Mind"* comes from Japanese Zen Buddhism and refers to the attitude of maintaining an open and receptive mind, free of preconceptions and judgments, like that of a beginner seeing things for the first time. This approach allows you to experience and learn more deeply and authentically.

quality of its interactions and the strength of its internal community.

From the very beginning, David knew that a strong organizational culture would be the backbone of Nubank's success. With this clear vision in mind, in addition to the initial Pitch Deck, he created a second document called the *Values Deck*. This carefully refined compendium, developed with his co-founders, encapsulated the principles that would guide the company from its earliest days into the future.

The Values Deck is not just a set of pretty words. It is a living document that David personally presents to every new employee during onboarding.[223] This allows him to connect directly with new generations of Nubankers and emphasize the importance of culture within the company. Every team member hears, in David's own voice, *the values that define what it means to succeed at Nubank—and what it means not to.*[224]

NU Rituals

Nubank has cultivated a vibrant and dynamic organizational culture that fosters innovation, collaboration, and employee well-being. Through a series of internal rituals and practices, they ensure that these values remain active and ingrained in daily life—not just as attractive signs and slogans on the wall (which, incidentally, they do have, and in abundance).

---

[223] Onboarding is the process by which new employees are introduced and integrated into a company. It covers the entire process from the initial legal and tax procedures to monitoring progress throughout the incorporation period. This is where new employees acquire the knowledge, skills and behaviors necessary to become effective organizational members and insiders. This process is also called "induction".

[224] Cfr. Op.Cit. Trava, Oswaldo, Podcast. Abr. 2020.

Cultural Onboarding
The First Step towards Nubank Culture

From day one, new employees are immersed in an induction program that covers not only the technical aspects of their roles but also the essence of Nubank's culture and values. Company leaders share inspiring stories and examples of how these values are put into practice every day.

This ensures that all Nubankers, regardless of their role, understand and align with the company's mission and core principles from the very start. By involving leaders in this process, the importance of organizational culture is reinforced, motivating new team members to actively contribute to Nubank's growth and evolution.

All Hands Meetings
Transparency as a Pillar

These regular meetings bring the entire team together, either in person or virtually, to discuss recent achievements, challenges, and future goals. They foster transparency and ensure everyone remains aligned with Nubank's mission and objectives.

Keeping everyone on the same page strengthens the sense of community and shared purpose within the company. Open and continuous communication allows Nubank to adapt quickly to changes, stay focused on its goals, and continue driving innovation in the competitive financial market.

Nubank Way Week
A Week of Innovation and Collaboration

During this special week, activities, workshops, and talks are organized to reinforce the company's culture. These initiatives emphasize collaboration, innovation, and diversity, fostering an environment that supports both personal and professional growth.

Frequent Feedback
Continuous Improvement

At Nubank, continuous feedback is a cornerstone of the culture. Employees are encouraged to give and receive feedback regularly, fostering an environment of ongoing improvement and mutual respect.

Recognitions and Celebrations
Valuing the Best in Us

Nubank celebrates achievements and recognizes employees who embody its values. These acknowledgments range from shout-outs in meetings to formal awards, ensuring that effort and dedication are always appreciated and never go unnoticed.

Well-being Rituals
Caring for Body and Mind

The company offers programs and activities that support physical and mental well-being, including meditation sessions, yoga, and flexible workspaces. Employee well-being is a top priority, and these initiatives reflect that commitment.

Innovation Spaces
The Idea Laboratory

Hackathons[225] and other innovation events give employees the opportunity to work on creative projects and experiment with new ideas. These initiatives foster a culture of continuous innovation, helping keep Nubank at the forefront of the financial sector.

These rituals and practices not only promote Nubank's values but also deeply embed them into the daily lives of each employee. In doing so, Nubank ensures that its culture remains strong and vibrant, creating an environment where innovation and collaboration thrive.

Experience Over Time

To define the type of talent needed to become a Nubanker, the search focused on people with specific characteristics—not so much on their educational background, but on their mindset for learning and certain key behaviors. *We wanted employees who were committed to our long-term vision; we were not looking for short-term hires or mercenaries.* However, attracting the right people was only part of the challenge: leadership development was equally important, particularly because we sought to bring in

---

[225] A hackathon is an intensive event, usually of short duration (it can last from a few hours to several days), in which programmers, designers, software developers and other technology professionals come together to collaborate on the development of innovative technological projects. The term "hackathon" is a combination of "hack" (in the sense of exploring and experimenting with technology) and "marathon" (marathon). The objective is to promote innovation, reinforce networking, solve specific problems and strengthen the culture of collaboration and teamwork.

a lot of young talent early in their careers. We aimed to cultivate resilient leaders.

As the company grew, they were involved in various formal and informal exercises to assess the state of the organizational culture. Regular meetings were organized to share stories about failures and to foster an environment where taking risks was encouraged. Everyone in the company was held to a high-performance standard, supported by solid incentive packages based on shared goals, encompassing senior management to the lowest levels of the organization.

As the company grew, various formal and informal efforts were made to assess and strengthen the organizational culture. Regular meetings were held where employees shared stories of their failures to encourage risk-taking and innovation. Everyone in the company, from senior management to entry-level employees, was held to high-performance standards, supported by strong incentive packages tied to shared goals.

However, certain shortcomings began to emerge, stemming from a belief that Nubank had to remain independent and different from others in the sector. There was a noticeable hesitation toward hiring people with experience in banking or financial institutions.

This desire to do things differently led us to almost overlook—or at least undervalue—professional experience.

David later reflected on this:

We were very mindful of diversity on our teams—diversity in every sense—but one area where we fell short was in experience. I was somewhat rigid in that regard; if someone came from banking, I did not want them on the team. That caused us problems. We moved more slowly and made mistakes we could have avoided if we had known better.

For example, it took us nearly three years to figure out how to manage collections from customers who were late on payments. We tried to reinvent the wheel. If we had brought in someone from the industry who was an expert, they could have told us in just a few hours what worked and what did not.[226]

In an interview, Cristina commented:

Is there something I would change?

Well, I think we took too long to find the right HR person—someone who was highly skilled, very competent, and had a lot of experience. We should have done it much sooner; we delayed too long in seeking them out.

We spent many years with a beginner's mindset, which we valued greatly; but we eventually realized that there needs to be a balance between leveraging enriching experience and maintaining that beginner's

---

[226] Op.Cit. Trava, Oswaldo, Podcast. Abr. 2020.

mindset, which helps us see things more simply.[227]

Organizational Structure

Nubank operates with a highly agile organizational structure, specifically designed to support its rapid growth while maintaining a strong focus on innovation and customer service.

The company is divided into 9 main areas and 26 sub-areas. (See Annex 3)

The Board

David had a clear vision of the gaps that needed to be filled to successfully establish Nubank. His first step was to find two partners who could address the most critical aspects of his emerging idea: banking expertise and technological know-how to build the company's entire infrastructure. These needs were well met by Cristina and Edward.

However, beyond the founding team, another crucial area that required attention was the selection of shareholders and directors:

---

[227] Suarez, Karem. Entrevista. Jun 2024. "De Cero a Billones, la HISTORIA REAL de Nubank contada por David y Cristina Junqueira". https://www.youtube.com/watch?v=1tMJYqgQbe0

MANAGEMENT AND OPERATION

The board should be your advisors, your coaches—those who, with their experience and knowledge, will help fill in the gaps you may have. The strategy is to build a very diverse board.

David examined the Cap Table—Capitalization Table[228] to see who his investors were and selected those who could bring the most valuable experience to Nubank.

If your board members all have similar interests and experience, you are wasting your shares; you are diluting yourself for nothing.[229]

Nubank's Board of Directors consists of 9 members,[230] most of whom are independent. Board members are appointed for one-year terms and can be re-elected at the end of their term. (See Annex 4)

---

[228] The Cap Table is an abbreviation of "Capitalization Table", it is a document that details the ownership structure of the company. This document is essential for both startups and public companies, although its complexity may increase as the company grows and more rounds of financing are made or more shares are issued. It contains the names of the shareholders, what type of shares they have, the number, percentage of ownership, valuation, and dilution.

[229] Cfr. Morris, Nigel. Entrevista con David Vélez. Fintech Nexus. Jun 2022. "How this Digital Bank Brought Millions of People into the Financial System, Nubank (Full Session)" https://www.youtube.com/watch?v=yXLWiqPEt6U

[230] NU International. Board of Directors.
https://www.investidores.nu/en/governance/board-of-directors/

Ingenious Path to Profit

The NU Model

In an interview, David shared what he considered to be Nubank's simple secret:

> *The trick is that our operational costs are 20 times lower than those of traditional banks.*[231]

Nubank's business model and growth have become a remarkable academic case. Their revenues have grown quarter by quarter since the beginning, though they only managed to generate profits in the third quarter of 2022, nine years after their founding.

In the third quarter of 2022, Nubank posted a net profit of $7.8 million. By the first quarter of 2024, that number had surged to $379 million.

In 2023, Nubank reported total revenues of $8.03 billion, with a net profit of $1.031 billion, despite their ongoing investments to solidify their growth across Latin America.

This success stems from a strategy executed with patience and tight operational control. Nubank focuses on taking care of

---

[231] Cfr. Caracol Television. Los Informantes TV. Entrevista. Oct. 2023. https://www.facebook.com/CaracolTV/videos/el-colombiano-más-rico-del-mundo-david-David-la-mente-maestra-tras-nubank/863596941744570/

its customers and steadily expanding its user base. Ultimately, it is a volume-based strategy: while the income per customer may not be very high, it becomes substantial when multiplied by tens of millions.

This focus on customer experience and sustained growth has propelled Nubank to remarkable success. By keeping fees low and providing accessible, efficient banking services, they have built a loyal and expanding customer base. This approach has transformed Nubank into a model of how a fintech can challenge—and even surpass—traditional financial giants.

As the number of customers increases while other variables remain constant, profitability eventually surpasses the break-even point. Nubank achieved this in the third quarter of 2022. At that point, a critical mass of customers began to grow exponentially, attracting even more users. This large customer base enables Nubank to offer a wide range of services, further diversifying its revenue streams.

Nubank's internal analyses reveal that customers gradually increase their spending over time. Initially, they spend modestly, but as time passes, their spending grows, boosting revenues from interchange fees with merchants.

This steady, sustained growth is central to Nubank's strategy. By focusing on providing exceptional service and building a loyal customer base, they have managed not only to attract but also to retain their users.

The Credit Card Business

Nubank's core strategy is to keep as many active customers as possible, multiplying their revenue by what each customer generates through card usage, while maintaining tightly controlled operating costs.

Within this model, Nubank has several sources of income:

- **Interest from Loans and Credit Cards**: Nubank generates revenue by charging interest on credit card balances and personal loans provided to customers.
- **Transaction Fees**: While Nubank does not charge fees for its basic services, it earns money through transaction fees paid by merchants when customers use their cards for purchases.
- **Investment Products**: Nubank offers products like NuConta and NuInvest, which generate income through fees and commissions tied to these investment and savings services.
- **Interest from Deposits**: Nubank also earns revenue from the interest on deposits that customers hold in their accounts.
- **Insurance and Other Financial Products**: The company offers additional financial products, such as insurance, which contribute to its overall revenue.
- **Partnerships and Strategic Alliances**: Nubank collaborates with other companies to provide exclusive promotions and services, often sharing revenue generated through these partnerships.

David commented on this:

> *Our business model is fundamentally different from that of traditional banks. Most banks make money from customers who never fully pay off their balances and simply continue making minimum monthly payments—essentially encouraging people to accumulate debt.*
>
> *While we actively encourage customers to use their cards, our goal is for them to pay off their entire balance on time.*
>
> *In an ideal world, we would rely solely on revenue from merchants.*
>
> *We view ourselves more as a payments company than a financing company.*

On another occasion, David reaffirmed:

> *Our initial target customers were actually "transactors" rather than "revolvers."*
>
> *We specifically focus on transactors because they are more capital-efficient.*
>
> *Currently, 91% of our customers pay their balances in full and on time (transactors), while 9% carry balances from month to month (revolvers). Typically, in the market, these figures are closer to 70% and 30%, respectively.*

David elaborated on this further:

Our late fees and interest rates are generally comparable to those of traditional banks. We do not want our customers using our credit lines to finance their payments on other cards.

In fact, when customers use a credit line as a financing vehicle for their overall obligations, it introduces excessive risk and leads to significant losses.

We experimented with offering better rates to high-performing customers but found no evidence of price elasticity. Good customers pay off their balances regardless of the interest rates offered to them.

Nubank uses MasterCard as its payment processor.

As illustrated in the following image (not actual Nubank data), the average issuer earns a significant percentage of each transaction made with its card, while another portion goes to the acquirer. Networks and payment processors typically take the smallest percentage. Generally, fees are based on a percentage of the transaction amount, with some merchants also incurring a fixed fee per transaction, though this is not shown here.

The following example is for illustration purposes only, showing a hypothetical $50 e-commerce transaction and approximately what each party involved earns. Assuming a general card usage fee of about 3.5%, the merchant would pay around $1.75 per transaction. Of that amount, the issuer—in this case, potentially Nubank—would receive $1.00, or 57% of the total fee. The acquirer, which is the merchant's bank, would take

35% of the fee, or $0.61, with the remaining amounts distributed among the other involved parties.

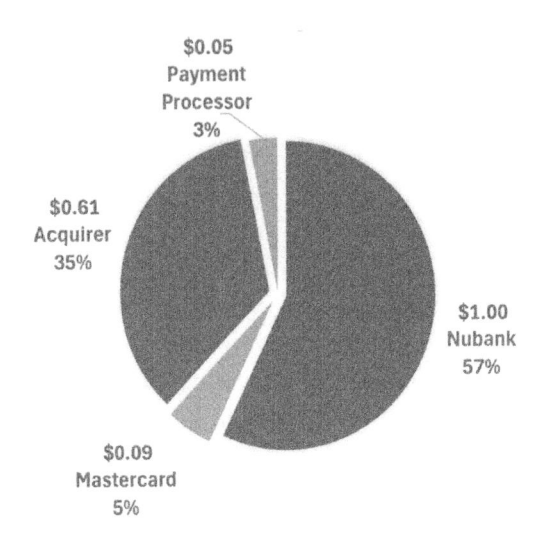

Pie chart:
- $0.05 Payment Processor 3%
- $0.61 Acquirer 35%
- $1.00 Nubank 57%
- $0.09 Mastercard 5%

Note: The percentages are concerning the 4 participants in the distribution of the 3.5% commission.

Interchange Fees

The credit card ecosystem is extremely complex, with processors charging hundreds of fees that vary based on a wide range of circumstances. To complicate matters further, many players are involved, each wanting a share of the commission pie. This has been a highly lucrative business over the years, but it is now evolving with the advent of simpler technologies and the widespread use of the Internet, which serves as a global omnipresent network. Before the Internet, dedicated connections were required at each store to process these transactions, often via phone lines. As a result, the payment system is becoming "less of a business" than it once was. Adding to this shift is stricter regulation aimed at curbing the high commissions that were once charged—fees that could reach up to 9% of a sale. Increased competition and regulation have significantly lowered these fees, which now average around 1.36% per transaction in many countries,[232] although in Europe, the average is only 0.36%.[233]

In a typical transaction between a consumer and a merchant, with credit card approval, at least eight different "gears" need to synchronize for the process to work. The fact that we can use our credit cards at virtually any store in our city—or anywhere in the world—is a technological marvel that brings enormous benefits. However, nothing comes without cost; there is always a price to pay for this convenience.

For businesses to accept credit card payments, they must usually sign up with a card processing service, and there are many to choose from. While new alternatives have simplified the process, for clarity, it is worth detailing the traditional services and entities involved.

---

[232] Cfr. Páez, Alejandro. Crónica, Nacional. Sep 2023. "Mexicanos pagan 6 veces más por uso de tarjetas que en Europa: Cofece".
https://www.cronica.com.mx/nacional/mexicanos-pagan-6-veces-tarjetas-europa-cofece.html#

[233] Sobrino, Ricardo. Cinco Días. El País. Jun 2024 "¿Cuánto le cuesta a un comercio el pago con tarjeta? ¿Qué bancos aplican las mayores comisiones?"
https://cincodias.elpais.com/mercados-financieros/2024-07-01/comisiones-bancarias-este-es-el-coste-para-los-comercios-de-recibir-pagos-con-tarjeta.html

Credit Card Payment Process

As mentioned, several actors and technologies collaborate in the credit card payment process to ensure secure and efficient transactions. From the cardholder initiating the purchase to the merchant, acquirer, and issuer managing authorization and settlement, each component plays a vital role. Card networks and payment processors facilitate communication and security, while payment gateways enable online transactions to be processed similarly to in-store transactions. This interconnected ecosystem is essential to modern commerce.

1. **Cardholder:** The credit card user who initiates a purchase.
2. **Merchant or Establishment:** The physical or online store where the purchase takes place.
3. **Point of Sale Terminal (POS):** The electronic device used by the merchant to read the card and send and receive transaction data. Acquiring banks typically provide POS terminals to merchants.
4. **Payment Gateway:** A digital version of a POS, enabling online merchants to accept card payments for customer purchases.
5. **Acquirer:** The financial institution that provides the merchant with the infrastructure to accept and process card payments.
6. **Issuer:** The financial institution that issues the credit card to the cardholder, authorizes the transaction, and charges the amount to the cardholder's account. It also pays the merchant, usually a few days later, for the purchase, minus the transaction fee.
7. **Card Network:** Facilitates communication between the acquirer and the issuer, setting the rules and standards for

transactions. These networks enable international transactions.
8. **Payment Processor (Payment Service Provider):** Handles data transmission and security, managing the authorization and settlement of transactions.

These services ensure that credit card payments are processed securely and efficiently. The merchant pays the fees involved in this process, which cover operational costs, fraud risks, and the profits of the companies involved. These interchange fees, set by the credit card networks, constitute the majority of the total processing fees.

In theory, consumers do not pay an additional percentage for processing payments with their cards. However, in some establishments, customers have been charged an extra fee for paying with a card. This was common with American Express, which had the highest commissions, prompting merchants to pass the cost on to customers. However, this practice has been declining due to American Express significantly reducing its commission rates and campaigns led by financial authorities.

As a result, merchants are responsible for paying the processing fees, which are set by card processors or card networks. These fees are part of a complex structure that takes into account regulations and economic conditions.

Payment Processing Fees Structure

Each provider has its own method for charging fees, but interchange fees remain consistent across the board. What sets providers apart is how they apply their profit margins. When a customer pays with a debit or credit card, the bank that issued the card receives a portion of the transaction, known as the interchange fee (or "wholesale" processing fee). This fee is designed to cover the bank's operational costs, fraud risk, and profit.

Importance of Interchange Fees

Interchange fees make up the bulk of the total credit card processing costs. These fees vary based on the type of card and the category of the transaction. Credit card networks such as Visa, MasterCard, Discover, and American Express each set their own interchange fee programs, each with a unique structure.

Interest Income

Like other players in the credit card processing ecosystem, issuing banks can generate substantial revenue from interchange fees on each credit card transaction. Merchants typically pay fees of around 2-3%, which are divided among the banks, card networks, and processors.

Additionally, banks earn interest income from the outstanding balances paid by consumers, commonly referred to as the Annual Percentage Rate (APR).

As of the first quarter of 2024, Nubank had 41.2 million active credit card customers.

Nubank also offers a debit account with no maintenance or usage fees, allowing customers to save money. The advantage is that Nubank pays an annual interest rate that is higher than the average rate offered by other banks—a strategy that has since been adopted by many of its global competitors.

In practice, when a bank or financial institution receives deposits from savers, it commits to paying them an interest rate. Simultaneously, the institution provides loans to borrowers at a higher interest rate. The difference between these two rates is known as the "Net Interest Margin" (NIM), representing the profit the institution earns through financial intermediation. This margin is essential for the bank's profitability, as it helps cover operating costs and generates additional income. Thus, the NIM becomes a key indicator of a bank's efficiency and financial management.

Delinquency Rate

Nubank's credit delinquency rate is 6.3%, roughly 10% lower than that of its local competitors in Brazil. A few years ago, Brazil's average delinquency rate was lower, around 5.7%.[234] By

---

[234] Cfr. Parra-Bernal, et al. Reuters. Sep 2016. "Tasa de morosidad y nuevos créditos en Brasil se mantienen estables en agosto".
https://www.reuters.com/article/idUSKCN11Y2CX/

comparison, in the United States, the credit card delinquency rate was approximately 3.16% during the last quarter of 2023.[235]

These figures highlight a clear difference in delinquency levels between markets, reflecting not only the distinct economic conditions of each region but also the varying strategies and policies financial institutions use to manage credit risk.

While calculating the delinquency rate in Brazil is no simple task, it is undeniable that delinquency levels remain exceptionally high. The annual penalty rate for delinquent credit in Brazil is approximately 431%, the highest in the Americas. This staggering figure underscores the severity of the issue and the immense challenges faced by borrowers in the country.

Although calculating the delinquency rate in Brazil[236] is no easy task, it is undeniable that delinquency is extremely high. The delinquency penalty rate is approximately 431% annually,[237] the highest in all of America. This astonishing figure highlights the severity of the problem and the challenges borrowers face in the South American country.

---

[235] Cfr. Federal Reserve Bank of New York. Feb 2024. Press Release. "Credit Card and Auto Loan Delinquencies Continue Rising; Notably Among Younger Borrowers".
https://www.newyorkfed.org/newsevents/news/research/2024/20240206
[236] The comparison of the cost of risk, default rate, versus the market is done in a similar way, using NU according to the old write-off methodology versus the Brazilian system adjusted for the same income distribution of the NU portfolio in a lagged manner (e.g. , adjusted for growth).
[237] Cfr. Página12. Ene 2024. Artículo: "Empieza a regir en Brasil el límite a los intereses de las tarjetas de crédito" https://www.pagina12.com.ar/700707-empieza-a-regir-en-brasil-el-limite-a-los-intereses-de-las-t#:~:text=Según%20los%20últimos%20datos%20del,registra%20mayores%20indices%20de%20morosidad.

Capitalization

To launch their venture, Nubank's co-founders needed a significant amount of capital: specifically, $2.25 billion to sustain the company for its first nine years. By 2024, Nubank was generating $8 billion in revenue, showcasing remarkable growth.

Throughout the funding rounds, the money was not as crucial for growth, as the company was already generating revenue. Instead, it was essential for Nubank's capitalization. Customers were joining in large numbers, and the business model was working perhaps even better than the founders had anticipated.

In line with David's goal of attracting *smart money*, Nubank accepted investments from strategic partners like Tencent. Although Tencent's contribution was only $300 million, the real value lay in their expertise, particularly their vast experience with payment systems in China. This partnership not only strengthened Nubank's financial position but also brought invaluable knowledge and strategies, which were critical for its expansion and market consolidation.

The initial seed capital that fueled Nubank's launch came from Sequoia and Kaszek, totaling $2 million. Subsequent capital infusions were made through various funding rounds (see Appendix 5).

During the search for initial funding, David was the sole founder. With his extensive experience in investment funds, particularly at Sequoia, he was not an easy target for negotiations.

As the saying goes, *It takes one to know one*. The negotiation process was swift and mutually satisfactory, especially for David, who, with his industry knowledge, likely secured a highly favorable deal. While he may have made some concessions, it was undoubtedly a *perfect* negotiation for all parties involved.

Typically, negotiations between founders and their initial investors result in giving up 10% to 20% of the company's equity.[238]

It is hard to overlook the fact that David likely saw Sequoia's investment as a powerful calling card to attract other investors. Having Sequoia on board gave Nubank invaluable legitimacy. David understood that Sequoia's backing would open doors and instill confidence in other potential investors.

When it came time to approach Kaszek, Sequoia's involvement made the investment proposition even more attractive.

Was it a good deal for Sequoia to trust David? That initial $1 million investment from Sequoia grew to nearly $3 billion—an extraordinary return. By 2024, Sequoia held the largest stake in Nubank, with 6.81% of the shares.

The IPO, often seen as the culmination of the capital-raising journey, allowed Nubank to sell 289.15 million shares, raising $2.6 billion.

With each funding round and the eventual IPO, the ownership stakes of the founders and early investors were

---

[238] Fleitmann, Maximilian, Base Templates. Ago 2023 "How Much Equity to Give Away in Seed Round". https://www.basetemplates.com/blog/how-much-equity-to-give-away-in-seed-round

diluted. However, the value of each remaining stake continued to rise. By July 2024, Nubank had 4.874 billion shares[239] (Diluted Average Shares),[240] and each had an average value of $12.37, which equated to a market value of approximately $59.3 billion.

David holds approximately 17% of the company.

To protect his position, David retained "super-voting shares," granting him 75% of the voting power in Nubank.

These super-voting shares give David more voting power per share than regular shares, allowing him to maintain substantial control over the company's decisions even if he does not hold a majority of the total shares. This ensures that the founders' vision and long-term strategy remain secure.

A notable example of this structure can be seen in companies like Alphabet Inc. (Google's parent company), where the founders hold enhanced voting rights to maintain control over the company.

---

[239] Yohoo!Finance. NU Holdings Ltd. Breakdow. Jun 2024. https://finance.yahoo.com/quote/NU/financials

[240] Diluted Average Shares includes not only outstanding common shares, but also the dilutive effect of financial instruments convertible into common shares. These may include Stock Options, Warrants, Convertible Notes, and Convertible Preferred Stock. The purpose of this distinction is to provide a broader view of the total number of shares that could be outstanding if all of these instruments were converted into common shares.

Financing

Each of Nubank's investment rounds was filled with challenges and moments of uncertainty. While securing financing often seemed like it would be straightforward, unexpected complications would arise, sometimes at the very last moment. Fortunately, a committed investor always stepped forward with the decisive words, *let's do it*. Despite these hurdles, the team never lost their optimism or the belief that everything would work out in the end.

The $2 million in seed capital they initially received was managed with great care, but it was not enough to fund the vast project they envisioned. To reach their ambitious goals, Nubank needed far more resources than they had first anticipated.

With that $2 million, Nubank was able to launch its credit card. The remarkable part was that, despite the challenges and expenses involved, they did not even exhaust all of the funds. This efficient use of resources not only brought their first product to market but also showcased the team's ability to maximize every dollar invested.

Each subsequent round of funding followed a similar pattern of tension followed by eventual success. Led by David, the Nubank team consistently proved their resilience and their knack for attracting the right investors.

Investment Rounds

Nubank needed to secure capital to launch its operations, with the initial funding provided by David Vélez. This was followed by a seed round, financed by Sequoia Capital and Kaszek Ventures, in exchange for a portion of the company's shares. The first major contribution from external investors came in 2014 during a Series A funding round, which raised $14.3 million and was again led by Sequoia Capital and Kaszek Ventures. This funding was critical for scaling operations and solidifying Nubank's market presence.

The purpose of investment rounds is to strengthen the company and enable it to scale its business.

At the start of a business, the first shares issued are called Common Shares or Founders' Shares, which are distributed among the founders and initial shareholders. To begin operations, a Seed Round or Pre-Seed round is necessary to secure the initial capital needed to test the concept and develop a minimum viable product (MVP). For Nubank, this MVP was the NU credit card.

During the Seed Round, the company can either use existing Common Shares or create new shares with a special rights structure known as Preferred Shares. Preferred Shares differ from Common Shares by offering negotiable terms that accommodate different types of investors. However, issuing Preferred Shares dilutes the ownership of each shareholder.

From that point forward, all newly issued shares will be Preferred Shares, categorized by series (Series A, Series B, Series C, etc.). This structure creates a clear and organized framework for managing investments, rights, and expectations among the various participants in the company's growth and development.

The number of share series a company plans to issue over time depends on its evolving needs. All new series must be authorized by the company's board of directors. This process continues until the company ultimately decides to go public.

Each time a new series of shares (Series B, Series C, etc.) is issued, additional shares are created and added to the total existing shares. This increase in the total number of shares reduces the ownership percentage of the existing shareholders, including holders of both common and preferred shares. This dilution occurs because while the total number of shares grows, individual ownership percentages shrink unless shareholders purchase shares from the new series.

For example, if a startup has issued 1,000 common shares, representing 100% ownership of the company, and then conducts an investment round issuing 200 Series A shares, the following calculations would apply:

a) Total shares: 1,000 (common shares) + 200 (Series A shares) = 1,200 shares
b) New ownership percentage for common shares: 1,000 / 1,200 = 83.33% (down from 100% to 83.33%)
c) Ownership percentage for Series A shares: 200 / 1,200 = 16.67%
d) Pre-money valuation of the company (before the round): $8,000
e) Value per share before the round: $8,000 / 1,000 = **$8 per share**

f) Capital raised in the round: $3,000
g) Post-money valuation of the company: $8,000 (pre-money value) + $3,000 (capital raised) = $11,000
h) Value per share after the round: $11,000 / 1,200 = **$9.16 per share**

Dilution is a natural part of a startup's financing process. With each investment round, new funds and investors come on board, leading to the issuance of new shares and, as a result, the dilution of existing holdings. However, the aim is for the company's value to grow with each round, so that despite the percentage dilution, the absolute value of the founders' and early investors' holdings increases.

This growth in both the company's value and the number of shares makes each financing round a strategic step toward the business's consolidation and expansion. As the company advances and proves its viability and market potential, the rise in its valuation compensates for the dilution, ultimately benefiting all shareholders. Each investment round not only provides the capital needed to fuel growth but also strengthens confidence in the company's vision and strategic direction.

In an official communication commemorating its first 10 years, David wrote:

> *I also wanted to recognize the entrepreneur: this journey has been full of pain, sweat, and tears. It takes strong conviction to keep going in the face of macro-crises and detractors.*
>
> *As Albert Einstein supposedly said: "Everybody knew it was impossible until a fool*

who didn't know came along and did it." Be that fool.[241]

Funding the Future

For their first Series A round, the Nubank team approached potential investors with *frio na barriga* (butterflies in their stomachs) and an ambitious goal: to grow from 12 customers (themselves) in 2013 to 1 million by 2019. However, most investors they pitched to were skeptical and declined to participate. As was often the case, it was only after meeting with the final investor that they finally secured a yes. That investor took the risk and secured $17 million for them. By 2019, Nubank had surpassed 20 million customers.

Investors initially struggled to see the potential in Nubank's business model. Only those who recognized the long-term value of investing in such a disruptive venture dared to take the leap. None of the major investors have regretted it; in fact, their expectations have been far exceeded.

David reflected on this:

> *When we started Nubank, we wanted it to be a lifelong project, and every decision we make aligns with that vision. If your goal is to sell to a big bank within three years, you have to make entirely different choices.*

---

[241] Op Cit. NU, Blog. "NU cumple 10 años de desafiar el sistema financiero"

> *I believe our investors understand this. Not a single board member is pressuring us to sell or go public.*

As previously mentioned, Nubank completed 10 additional funding rounds beyond its Seed Capital, raising a total of $2.25 billion. These rounds included significant milestones:

1. **Series D in December 2016**: Nubank raised $179 million, led by DST Global. At that time, the company had 1 million credit card customers and was still experiencing rapid growth. By 2019, Nubank had doubled its revenue and was adding around 40,000 customers per day, reaching 19.7 million customers—more than three times its customer base in 2018.[242]

2. **Series E in February 2018**: Led by DST Global, Nubank raised $329 million. This round brought the company's valuation to $1 billion, officially making it a Unicorn.[243]

3. **October 2018**: Tencent Holdings invested $419 million and also purchased shares from an existing shareholder for an additional $90 million.

The **Series G** round was split into 3 parts: G1, G2, and G3:

> *With these two extensions, Nubank's Series G round raised a total of $1.15 billion, marking the*

---

[242] Silva, G. Feb 2020. "Balanço 2019: um ano que vai para a história do Nubank" -- Fala, Nubank. https://blog.nubank.com.br/balanco-nubank-2019/
[243] Wood, Sophia. Latam List. Mar 2018. "Nubank raises US$150M, becomes Brazil's third unicorn". https://latamlist.com/nubank-raises-us150m-becomes-brazils-third-unicorn/

largest private capital raise by a Latin American technology company at that time.[244]

On October 27, 2021, Nubank filed for its Initial Public Offering (IPO). On December 9, 2021, it officially went public. The IPO price was estimated between $8 and $9 per share,[245] with the company selling 289 million shares[246] to raise approximately $3 billion. By then, Nubank had 48 million customers. On its first day of trading, the company's shares rose by 15%, pushing its valuation to $45 billion.

Nubank has already reached profitability in Brazil, generating $4 billion in annual revenue. They have achieved impressive operational efficiency, enabling them to increase sales without proportionally increasing operational expenses. This efficiency has set them apart from other tech companies still struggling to find that balance. In one year, Nubank's growth soared by 170% compared to the previous year.

Nubank's IPO in December 2021 was a significant milestone, but the world changed soon after with the onset of the Russia-Ukraine war in 2022. Inflation soared, and interest rates began to rise rapidly, dampening investors' enthusiasm for high-growth companies. Like many tech firms, Nubank's shares experienced a decline.

Despite these challenges, Nubank remains a dominant force in the financial sector. Approximately 73.82% of its shares

---

[244] Nubank. https://blog.nu.com.mx/nubank-cierra-una-segunda-ampliacion-de-su-ronda-serie-g-elevandola-a-us-115-mil-millone/
[245] Formato F1.
[246] Wood, Sophia. Latam List. Mar 2018. "Nubank raises US$150M, becomes Brazil's third unicorn". https://latamlist.com/nubank-raises-us150m-becomes-brazils-third-unicorn/

are held by 800 institutions, reflecting sustained confidence and interest in its business model and growth potential. See Appendix 6 for a table of the major shareholders
.

Challenges

A Rocky Road

Since Nubank began 11 years ago, the landscape in which it operates has changed drastically. In the beginning, there was a significant opportunity because credit cards were expensive and widely disliked by consumers. With the introduction of its iconic purple card, Nubank not only disrupted the market but also achieved remarkable growth. However, the current environment is very different. Nubank now faces fierce competition—not only from emerging startups but also from traditional banks that have evolved and now offer much more customer-friendly products.

Nubank was the first fintech to offer attractive interest rates to encourage savings among its customers. This strategy was highly successful and earned the company greater prestige, proving that Nubank was truly committed to improving customers' financial lives. However, this approach has since been adopted by nearly all new fintechs. Even some banks and brokerage firms, feeling the pressure and losing customers, have followed suit, so Nubank is no longer the only player offering competitive savings rates.

Nubank changed the rules of the game, and surprisingly, for the benefit of the entire industry and its customers, nearly everyone is now following its lead. While this has raised standards across the sector, it also means Nubank must continue innovating to stay ahead. The competitive environment now demands the same level of urgency and innovation that defined its early days.

Nubank faces several risks to its business. According to one of the F-1A forms filed with the SEC, the company has historically generated a significant portion of its income from credit card interchange fees (30%) and interest charged on credit cards (23%). These revenue streams could be impacted if regulators impose limits or if provisions such as Brazil's *Over-Indebtedness Law*[247] are implemented. This law not only encourages responsible financial and credit education but also pressures financial institutions to lower their rates and fees, potentially reducing profit margins. This could affect everything from commissions charged to merchants for credit card acceptance to interest on loans and late payment penalties.

We Are the Best

No one can deny that Nubank has achieved remarkable success; they are profitable and have built an enormous customer base, which provides a strong platform for expanding their services. However, David Vélez remains concerned that, with this evident success, the spark of innovation necessary for continued evolution could fade.

---

[247] The draft Super-indebtedness Law in Brazil, passed in 2021, and the one proposed in Chile seek to protect consumers from over-indebtedness through credit regulation, the promotion of financial education and the implementation of mechanisms for debt renegotiation. In both countries, it is guaranteed that debtors maintain sufficient resources to cover their basic needs after paying their debts, promoting responsible and transparent credit practices.

David explained:

> Perhaps the greatest threat we face is thinking we've already made it, that we've already won, that we are very good.
>
> (...) We have redefined what it means to be a new kind of bank, though we are more of a consumer platform than a traditional bank. We must move carefully, but in 5 or 10 years, we will be in more countries.
>
> (...) We must remember that we are still in the early minutes of the first half; we cannot rest on our laurels in these first minutes.[248]

For David, this presents a real challenge. The Nubank team, seeing their success in the headlines and the widespread presence of the purple card, could easily fall into the trap of complacency. Despite their rigorous hiring process, which focuses on clearly defining the type of people they need and carefully identifying the right profiles, there is still a risk that a sense of *mission accomplished* could weaken their drive to continually exceed expectations.

Nubank's greatest advantage is that there is still so much left to do.

The team operates in a continuous cycle of completing one task and immediately planning the next challenge. The

---

[248] Stebbings, Harry. Entrevista 20VC. E1059. Sep 2023. "David Velez: How AI Changes The Future of Fiinance".
https://youtu.be/as_jwyokTDI?si=BYdjebgg28wLZaRQ

mission is far from over; there are always more projects and goals on the horizon.

This vision of endless opportunities is key to sustaining the energy and focus needed for constant innovation.

Nubank is committed to preserving the sense of urgency that has driven them since day one, regardless of their success so far. For David, it is essential that everyone on the team maintains that hunger for improvement and growth, ensuring they do not stop until they have fully transformed the financial sector and beyond.

Strategic and Operational Risks

From the beginning, Nubank faced a range of strategic and operational risks that tested its ability to revolutionize the banking industry in Brazil. One of the biggest challenges was consumer distrust. Brazilians, accustomed to traditional banks, were initially skeptical of a fintech with no physical branches. David and his team quickly realized that offering an innovative service was not enough; they needed to earn the trust of a public that placed great value on stability and security in financial transactions. To do this, Nubank had to consistently prove that its platform was not only secure but also provided a level of convenience and accessibility that traditional banks could not match.

Another significant challenge was educating customers. Nubank sought to break entrenched banking habits by introducing the benefits of a digital-first service without hidden fees. But this was no easy feat. Consumers, long accustomed to the complexity and opacity of traditional banks—visiting branches, filling out forms, signing documents—were naturally wary of the idea of a fully online service. They felt that something was "missing"—there was no "formality," no physical documents or contracts to sign in front of a bank official. Yet Nubank remained firm, insisting that good service and reliability did not require these traditional formalities.

Nubank invested heavily in communication and awareness campaigns to educate the public about the NU model while ensuring an exceptional customer service experience. Their goal was to prove that digital banking could be secure, simple, and hassle-free, and that despite being digital, it was always available when you needed to speak with someone. It was digital, yet always present.

On the technological front, building a robust platform capable of handling millions of transactions securely and efficiently was a monumental challenge. Edward, the architect of Nubank's technology infrastructure, led a team that worked tirelessly to ensure the software operated seamlessly as the company scaled rapidly. Every update and new feature was meticulously designed to provide a flawless user experience while maintaining the highest security standards.

Integrating with existing banking systems and complying with Brazil's financial regulations presented numerous technical and bureaucratic obstacles. Nubank had to navigate a complex regulatory environment while ensuring that its innovations met the standards set by financial authorities. They succeeded in doing so, not only overcoming technological barriers but also fostering strong relationships with regulators. By demonstrating a commitment to compliance and the stability of the financial system, Nubank positioned itself more as an ally than a disruption.

Financial Regulation

Nubank's approach to regulation in the countries where it operates has always been one of deep respect and a commitment to full compliance. *We are like the front-row student who always wants to get an A+, who wants to know everything,*[249] David often says. This philosophy has shaped their relationship with regulators from the start.

When Nubank first engaged with regulators in Brazil, they approached with apprehension. David had been warned that they would face a rigid, unsympathetic regulator who might view their startup unfavorably. However, they were pleasantly surprised. Not only did the regulators like the idea, but they also encouraged them to move forward, noting that competition was beneficial and expressing discontent that 80% of the market was dominated by just five banks. While they insisted on full regulatory compliance, they also committed to helping Nubank meet those requirements.

At that time, no specific regulations gave Nubank an advantage for being a fintech, simply because there was no regulatory framework for such companies yet. What worked in their favor was the broader trend toward digitalization, especially

---

[249] De la C, Juan Carlos. Entrevista con David. Imagen Radio. May 2024. "Crecimiento de Nubank en México, Colombia y Brasil. https://youtu.be/wPUBO20vxJk?si=rwcEEy92HtYYtDvx

accelerated by the COVID-19 pandemic, which pushed people to seek digital solutions for managing their finances from home.

Navigating Regulation

Like any provider of financial products, Nubank had to ensure full compliance with local regulations—a particularly challenging task for a startup trying to innovate and offer non-traditional services. Initially, many critics argued that Nubank had unfair advantages due to the lack of specific fintech regulations. However, once they applied for a banking license, that argument faded. Nubank understood that greater regulation not only provided necessary control and protection for the financial system but also acted as a barrier to entry in an increasingly competitive market, ensuring that all players were held to the same standard.

Unlike regions such as the United States and Europe, where protecting established businesses and resisting financial innovation is common, countries like India, China, and Brazil have shown a more favorable attitude toward fintech. In Brazil, for instance, around 50% of the population is unbanked, and regulators are actively seeking to address this issue by promoting innovation and competition—an opportunity that Nubank has capitalized on to expand and offer inclusive services.

When faced with the challenge of reducing payment processing times for merchants, Nubank adopted a proactive and strategic approach. To navigate this and other potential regulatory changes, they established a dedicated team focused exclusively on regulation, tasked with monitoring developments and analyzing emerging trends.

This team not only ensures that Nubank is never caught off guard by regulatory changes but, perhaps more importantly, actively collaborates with regulators to help shape the regulatory environment. Their goal is to anticipate new regulations and adapt swiftly, minimizing operational disruptions while maximizing their ability to remain fully compliant.

This proactive approach perfectly reflects Nubank's philosophy of being the *front-row student, the eager beaver*. By staying ahead of the latest trends and regulations, Nubank not only safeguards its operations but also positions itself as a key collaborator in shaping the regulatory framework. This close, active relationship with regulators not only facilitates compliance but also contributes to creating a more favorable environment for financial innovation.

The Purple Revolution in Retrospective

In this work, three major themes are intricately woven together: David's life and his quiet, almost unnoticed preparation for his "final exam"; the valuable entrepreneurial lessons from Nubank's founding, offering insights for anyone looking to disrupt industries urgently needing "digital/tech transformation"; and the phenomenon of Nubank itself—a fintech venture that not only revolutionized traditional banking processes but also redefined customer service and care.

David, with his journey full of lessons and challenges, seemed to be in a constant state of preparation. Every experience, every challenge overcome, led him to a culminating point where he was ready to face the financial world. Unknowingly, every step in his life and career were lessons that, combined with his entrepreneurial spirit, innovative vision, and ability to surround himself with talent to multiply his potential, prepared him to create Nubank.

Each challenge David faced became a crucial piece of the puzzle that would ultimately form Nubank. His ability to learn from every situation, absorb knowledge, and apply it strategically gave him the tools needed to create a company that not only revolutionized banking in Brazil but also set new standards in the global financial industry.

Surrounded by a team of visionaries and experts, David envisioned a digital bank rooted in a culture of innovation. His disruptive approach and ability to look beyond traditional barriers transformed Nubank into a technological and financial powerhouse, challenging established giants and offering accessible, efficient financial services to millions.

The image of David versus Goliath that Vélez included in his initial pitch deck served as his inspiration against every obstacle, of which there were indeed many.

Nubank, meanwhile, is not just a symbol of technological innovation and disruption in traditional banking. It has also become a case study in the academic world, demonstrating how a company can transform a sector long dominated by entrenched incumbents. The key to its success lies in its customer-centric focus, with attention and care forming the core pillars of its operations.

This innovative approach presents itself as a model that could transform other sectors equally in need of renewal. Why not, for example, the insurance and hospital services sectors? Like banking before Nubank's arrival, these sectors are characterized by archaic processes and operational rules, a strong bureaucracy disguised as operational efficiency, and a lack of customer attention that has frustrated millions of clients for years. Hospital services and insurance are extremely expensive, with treatment that borders on contempt. The combination of major medical insurance and the services provided by hospitals is the best example of the urgent need for change.

Imagining a transformation in these sectors is not difficult. Insurance, with its complicated and often incomprehensible procedures, could greatly benefit from simplification and digitalization that puts the customer at the center. Similarly, hospital services, which often suffer from inefficiency and impersonal care, could experience a revolution by adopting technologies and processes that prioritize patient well-being and comfort.

David has already demonstrated with Nubank that it is possible to challenge and surpass established giants with a bold and innovative approach. The insurance and hospital sectors are ripe for a similar shake-up, one that places customer care and attention at the heart of their operations. Globally, these industries urgently need a transformation that not only modernizes their services but also humanizes their approach. Just as David aimed with Nubank at the banking sector, we find that the true revolution begins when the needs of people are listened to and responded to.

From its early steps to its meteoric rise, Nubank has redefined the banking landscape in Latin America. The story of Nubank is not merely one of financial, administrative, and corporate innovation; it is a testament to the power of vision and perseverance. David, Cristina, and Edward did not simply found a company—they sparked a movement that challenged and ultimately overcame the barriers of a banking system that had been rigid for centuries.

Annexes

Annex 1

Digital Banks by Foundation Date

#	Bank	Foundation Date	Nationality	Active	License	Number of Customers (millions)
1	Tinkoff	08/12/06	Russia	Yes	Yes	10
2	Simple	01/06/09	USA	No, 2021	No	0
3	Ally Bank	11/12/09	USA	Yes	Yes	9.6
4	Sofi	01/08/11	USA	Yes	Yes	5
5	N26	01/02/13	Germany	Yes	Yes	7
6	Kokoa	18/04/13	South Korea	Yes	Yes	14
7	Nubank	06/05/13	Brazil	Yes	Yes	100
8	Tandem Bank	01/11/13	UK	Yes	Yes	1
9	Atom Bank	01/04/14	UK	Yes	Yes	1.5
10	Starling Bank	01/06/14	UK	Yes	Yes	3.5
11	Bank Mobile	01/01/15	USA	Yes	Yes	2
12	Monzo	01/02/15	UK	Yes	Yes	6
13	Revolut	01/07/15	UK	Yes	Yes	28
14	Varo Money	01/07/15	USA	Yes	Yes	4
15	Judo Bank	22/03/16	Australia	Yes	Yes	0.15

Annex 2

Nubank Products Overview

#	Product Name	Description	Launch Date
1	Tarjeta de Crédito Nubank	Credit card with no fees, full control from the mobile app.	Sep 2014
2	Nubank Rewards	Rewards program that allows accumulating points for each purchase, redeemable for products and services.	2017
3	NuConta (Cuenta Digital)	Digital checking account with no maintenance fees, free transfers, and interest on the balance.	Oct 2017
4	Préstamos Personales	Personal loans with a completely digital application and management through the Nubank app.	2018
5	Caixinhas	Financial organization and planning tool to save money in a personalized way with returns.	2022

6	Nubank Auto	Car insurance with a 100% digital experience and 24-hour support.	2023
7	Nubank Lar Seguro	Customizable home insurance with a 100% digital experience.	2023
8	Nucoin	Free utility token as part of a loyalty program based on blockchain technology.	2023
9	Nubank Cripto	Cryptocurrency offering with 14 options available for trading, including USDC.	2023
10	NuConsignado	Payroll-deducted loans with guarantees, for public employees and pensioners.	2023
11	NU Limite Garantido	Tool to increase the credit card limit using invested amounts as collateral.	2023
12	Me Roubaram	Tool to quickly block cards or accounts in case of theft or loss.	2023
13	Alô Protegido	Feature to identify and block fraudulent calls.	2023

14	ETFs NU Renda Ibov Smart Dividendos	ETF tracking an index derived from Ibovespa focusing on companies that pay dividends.	2023
15	ETFs NU Ibov Smart Dividendos	ETF that reinvests dividends into the ETF itself to increase returns.	2023
16	Nubank Ultravioleta	Exclusive Black-type card with various benefits for high-income clients, including NuTag and Rappi Prime.	2023
17	Caixinhas SME	Financial organization and planning tool for SME clients.	2022 (expanded in 2023)
18	Nubank+	Benefits program with cashback, streaming access, free withdrawals, and payment assistant.	2024
19	Cuenta PJ	Bank account for small and medium-sized businesses.	2019
20	Tarjeta de Crédito PJ	Credit card for small and medium-sized businesses.	2019

Annex 3

Organizational Structure of Nubank

General Area	Sub-area	Description
Executive Management	CEO (Chief Executive Officer)	Responsible for the overall direction of the company.
	CGO (Chief Growth Officer)	In charge of operations in new countries.
	COO (Chief Operating Officer)	Responsible for daily operations and the implementation of the company's strategy.
	CFO (Chief Financial Officer)	Manages the company's finances, including financial planning and investor relations.
	CTO (Chief Technology Officer)	Leads technology efforts and product development.
	CRO (Chief Risk Officer)	Director of Risks. Responsible for identifying, assessing, and mitigating risks.
	CPO (Chief Product Officer)	Responsible for product development and management.

Product Development and Technology	Software Engineering	Develop and maintain Nubank's technological infrastructure.
	Product Design	Focus on user experience and interface design.
	Data Science and Analytics	Data analysts and scientists working on data-driven decision making.
Customer Service	Customer Support	Handle customer inquiries and issues through various channels such as chat, phone, and social media.
	Support Process Optimization	Continuously improve the efficiency and quality of customer support.
Operations	Transaction Management	Ensure the correct execution of all financial transactions.
	Regulatory Compliance	Ensure that Nubank complies with all applicable laws and regulations.
	Fraud Prevention	Teams dedicated to identifying and preventing fraudulent activities.

Marketing and Sales	Marketing Strategy	Develop campaigns to acquire and retain customers.
	Market Analysis	Conduct studies and analyses to better understand the market and customer needs.
	Communication and PR	Manage Nubank's public image and external communications.
Finance	Accounting and Corporate Finance	Manage internal financial aspects.
	Financial Planning and Analysis (FP&A)	Financial planning and analysis to support strategic decision making.
	Investor Relations	Manage communication and relationships with investors and shareholders.

Human Resources	Recruitment	Responsible for attracting and hiring talent.
	Development and Training	Programs for professional development and continuous training of employees.
	Benefits and Compensation Management	Handling employee benefits and compensation.

Legal and Compliance	Legal Advisory	Handle legal and contractual matters.
	Compliance and Regulation	Ensure all operations and products comply with laws and regulations.
Innovation and Strategy	Strategic Planning	Teams working on the long-term strategy of the company.
	Research and Development (R&D)	Projects for research and development of new technologies and products.

Annex 4

Members of the Board of NUBANK

Name	On the Board Since	Current Company	Position
David Vélez Osorno	Founder, Chairman, CEO	NU	Chief Executive Officer
Anita Mary Sands	Member, since Oct 2020	ServicesNow, JumpCloud, Circle Internet Financial, Cyderes	Member of various Boards
Daniel Krepel Goldberg	Member, since Apr 2021	Lumina Capital Management	Managing Partner and CIO
David Marcus	Member, since Mar 2023	Lightspark	CEO and Co-founder
Douglas Mauro Leone	Member, since 2016	Sequoia Capital	Partner
Jacqueline Dawn Reses	Member, since Mar 2021	Lead Bank	Chairwoman and Chief Executive Officer
Luis Alberto Moreno Mejía	Member, since Apr 2021	Allen & Co.	Managing Director
Rogério Paulo Calderón Peres	Member, Chairman Audit and Risk Committee	Alupar Investimentos S.A.	Member of the Board of Directors
Thuan Quang Pham	Member, since Sep 2022	Faire	CTO

Annex 5

Funding Rounds from 2014 to 2021

Series	Amount Raised (million USD)	Date	Round
A	17	Aug-14	Sequoia, Kaszek
B	47	May-15	TGM
C	99	Jun-16	Founders Fund
D	179	Dec-16	DTS Global
E	150	Feb-18	DTS Global
E1	90	Oct-18	Tencent
F	400	Jul-19	TCV
G1	400	Jan-21	GIC
G2	500	Jun-21	Berkshire Hathaway
G3	250	Jun-21	Sand Capital
Total	2,253		

Annex 6

Some of the Most Important Investors of NU

Investor	Shares (millions)	Position Value (USD)	% Change	% Ownership as of 5/26/24	% Shares Outstanding
Sequoia Capital Partners Inc.	251.9	$3,005,699,388	+8%	6.8%	Low
Tencent Holdings Ltd	244.7	$2,038,459,198	+8%	6.7%	Low
Capital Research Global Investors	202.6	$2,417,236,772	+7%	5.5%	Low
Baillie Gifford & Co.	169.5	$2,021,539,979	+6%	4.6%	Low
Berkshire Hathaway Inc.	107.1	$1,277,927,093	+4%	2.9%	Low
WCM Investment Management	100.0	$1,192,589,930	+3%	2.7%	Low
Sands Capital Management, LLC	88.6	$1,056,580,975	+3%	2.4%	Low
Jennison Associates LLC	87.2	$1,039,769,720	+3%	2.4%	Low
Technology Crossover Ventures	69.7	$831,840,843	+2%	1.9%	Low
Coatue Management, L.L.C.	62.8	$749,358,696	+2%	1.7%	Low

About the Author

Jorge Livingstone Vaught has extensive experience in technological innovation, business strategy, and process automation. He holds an MBA in Business Management from IPADE and graduated from ITAM with a degree in Business Administration, also earning a Specialization in Computer Systems from the same institution.

In the late 1990s, as Country Manager, Jorge introduced Gateway computers to Mexico. These were marketed as *computers with a first and last name, yours*, as they were 100% customizable to the customers' preferences, featuring the latest technology available at that time. His career includes a tenure at the Mexican Stock Exchange, where for 10 years he served as the Director of Technology and Innovation in the Money Market; completely redesigning the infrastructure and operational and communication applications of the Money Market with the Mexican interbank market.

Jorge has been an innovative entrepreneur, implementing digital solutions that have transformed processes and improved operational efficiency in various companies.

In the academic field, he has published multiple articles on technology and innovation, frequently contributing professionally on LinkedIn. In addition to being a dedicated educator, he has been active for over 30 years, teaching courses on technology, fintech, digital banking, and financial education at renowned universities.

Email: jorgelv@mac.com
LinkedIn: https://linkedin.com/in/jorge-livingstone

Printed in Great Britain
by Amazon